The Gift of Change

Change

Spiritual Guidance for a Radically New Life

MARIANNE WILLIAMSON

Element
An Imprint of HarperCollins*Publishers*
77–85 Fulham Palace Road,
Hammersmith, London W6 8JB

The website address is www.thorsonselement.com

and *Element* are trademarks of
HarperCollins*Publishers* Limited

First published in the US by HarperCollins*Publishers* 2004
This edition published by Element 2005

5 7 9 10 8 6 4

© Marianne Williamson 2004

Marianne Williamson asserts the moral right to
be identified as the author of this work

A catalogue record for this book
is available from the British Library

ISBN-13 978-0-00-719904-4
ISBN-10 0-00-719904-X

Printed and bound in Great Britain by
Creative Print and Design (Wales), Ebbw Vale

For my mother

Contents

Acknowledgments

Writing a book can take over your life for a while. To those who supported me while I wrote this one, I am deeply grateful: To Bob Barnett, whose steady hand has steered my literary career for years. I profoundly appreciate his sage and invaluable counsel, both on this book and on previous ones. I consider myself extremely fortunate to have his guidance in my life.

To Steve Hanselman, for welcoming me back to Harper-Collins and for making me feel like I belong there. I hope this book is worthy of his confidence and faith.

To Mickey Maudlin, for taking as much care with my nervous author's psyche as with my words. To Terri Leonard, Claudia Boutote, Jennifer Johns, Priscilla Stuckey, Lisa Spindler, and Jim Warner, thank you for your professional excellence and generous support.

To Andrea Cagan, for being the muse who once again came through for me, using her editorial and emotional genius to get me back on the literary track.

To Nancy Peske, whose editorial assistance was completely invaluable. I cannot overestimate her talents or her help to me. Whatever is good in this book is partly because of her. Whatever is not so good, is all because of me.

To Oprah Winfrey, for creating my national audience to begin with and for continuing to support my work. She has made a world of difference in my life, as she has in the lives of millions of others. In my heart I thank her constantly.

To Chalanda Sai Ma, for her light in my veins.

To Victoria Pearman, Diane Meyer Simon, Stacie Maier, Christen Brown, Suzannah Galland, Alyse Martinelli, Bonnie Raitt, Joycelyn Thompson, and Anne Lamott—for love and sisterhood.

To Richard Cooper, for reading my book, my mind, and my heart.

To Tammy Vogsland, Casey Palmer, Matthew Albracht, Marci Stassi, Mary Holloway, Andy Stewart, Debra Carter, Kristina Roenbeck, Maryvette, Helen Sushynska, and John Marusich, for their unique contributions to my life.

To my mother, for everything she is and has been and always will be for me.

And to my darling Emma, for filling my heart with a love that so matters. You are my biggest blessing.

To all of the above, my deep and abiding thanks. Particularly this time, I could not have done it without you.

Behold, I tell you a mystery: We shall not all sleep, but we shall all be changed—in a moment, in the twinkling of an eye, at the last trumpet. For the trumpet will sound, and the dead will be raised incorruptible, and we shall be changed.

—1 Corinthians 15:51–52, NKJV

The Challenge to Grow

*T*he times in which we live are difficult, more difficult than a lot of people seem willing to admit. There is an abiding sense of collective anxiety, understandable but not always easy to talk about.

When things aren't going well for you in your personal life, perhaps you call a friend or family member or go to a therapist or support group to process your pain. Yet when your feelings of upset are based on larger social realities, it's hard to know how to talk about them and to whom. When you're afraid because you don't know where your next paycheck is going to come from, it's easy to articulate; when you're worried about whether the human race is going to survive the next century, it feels odd to mention it at lunch.

And so, I think, there is a collective depression among us, not so much dealt with as glossed over and suppressed. Each of us, as individual actors in a larger drama, carries an imprint of a larger despair. We are coping with intense amounts of chaos and fear, both personally and together. We are all being challenged, in one form or another, to recreate our lives.

On the level of everyday conversation, we conspire with each other to pretend that things are basically okay, not because we think they are but because we have no way of talking together about these deeper layers of experience. If I tell you what happened in my personal life today, I might also mention how I am feeling about it, and both are considered relevant. But when it comes to our collective experience, public dialogue allows for little discussion of events of equally personal magnitude. "We accidentally bombed a school today, and fifty children died." How do we *feel* about that? Uh-oh, we don't go there. . . .

So we continue to talk mainly about other things, at a time when the news of the day is as critical as at any time in the history of the world. Not dealing with our internal depths, we emphasize external superficialities. Reports on the horrors of war appear intermittently between reports on box office receipts for the latest blockbuster movie and a Hollywood actress's vintage Valentino. I see the same behavior in myself, as I jump from writing about things that demand I dig deep to obsessively checking my e-mails for something light and fun to distract me. It's like avoidance behavior in therapy—wanting to share the gossip but not wanting to deal with the real, more painful issues. Of course we want to avoid the pain. But by doing so, we inevitably cause more of it.

That is where we are today. We are acting out our anger and fear because we are not facing the depth of our pain. And keeping the conversation shallow seems a prerequisite for keeping the pain at bay. Those who would engage in a deeper conversation are systematically barred from the mainstream: from newspapers and magazines, from TV, and especially from political power.

One night I was watching a news broadcast about the latest videotape purportedly sent by Osama bin Laden to an Arab television network. The focus of the American news story was not on bin Laden's message but rather on the technology by which

Americans had verified the recording. His message was too horrifying; it was as though we were trying to emotionally distance ourselves from it by having a beautiful news reporter discuss the technology of the tape rather than its contents.

Visiting a medical office one day recently, I asked my doctor, a member of the "greatest generation," how he had been feeling lately.

"Fine," he said. "How about you?"

"I'm okay," I said. "But I feel like everybody is freaking out on the inside these days; we're just not talking about it. I think the state of the world has us more on edge than we're admitting."

"I think that's true," he sighed. "Things would get bad before, but you always had a sense they would ultimately be okay. Now I don't necessarily feel that way . . ." His voice trailed off, his sadness obvious. As unhappy as he was with the state of the world, he seemed grateful I had brought it up. The fact that we go about our lives as though the survival of the world is not at stake is not the sign of a stiff upper lip. It is the sign, rather, of a society not yet able or willing to hold a conversation about its deepest pain.

We are being challenged by world events, by the tides of history, to develop a more mature consciousness. Yet we cannot do that without facing what hurts. Life is not a piece of tragic fiction, in which at the end of the reading we all get up and go out for drinks. All of us are actors in a great unfolding drama, and until we dig deep, there will be no great performances. How each of us carries out our role will affect the end of the play.

Who we ourselves become, how we grow and change and face the challenges of our own lives, is intimately and causally connected to how the world will change over the next few years. For the world is a projection of our individual psyches, collected on a global screen; it is hurt or healed by every thought we think. To whatever extent I refuse to face the deeper issues that hold me back, to that extent the world will be held back. And to whatever extent I find the miraculous key to the transformation of my own life, to that extent I will help change the world. That is what this book is about: becoming the change that will change the world.

Yet we seem to have great resistance to looking at our lives, and our world, with emotional honesty. And I think we are avoiding more than pain. We are avoiding the sense of hopelessness we *think* we will feel when confronted by the enormity of the forces that obstruct us. Yet, in fact, it's when we face the darkness squarely in the eye—in ourselves and in the world—that we begin at last to see the light. And that is the alchemy of personal transformation. In the midst of the deepest, darkest night, when we feel most humbled by life, the faint shadow of our wings begins to appear. Only when we have faced the limits of what we can do, does it begin to dawn on us the limitlessness of what God can do. It is the depth of the darkness now confronting our world that will reveal to us the magic of who we truly are. We are spirit, and thus we are more than the world. When we remember that, the world itself will bow to our remembrance.

Returning to Love

In 1978 I became a student of a self-study program of spiritual psychotherapy called *A Course in Miracles;* in 1992 I wrote a book of reflections on its principles called *A Return to Love.* Claiming no monopoly whatsoever on spiritual insight, the Course is a psychological mind training based on universal spiritual themes. It teaches people how to dismantle a thought system based on fear and replace it with a thought system based on love. Its goal is attaining inner peace through practicing forgiveness. You will notice it referred to throughout this book, and many of its teachings will be reflected in what I write. When there is no specific reference for quoted material or concepts from *A Course in Miracles* (published by the Foundation for Inner Peace), I have added an asterisk to mark *A Course in Miracles* principle.

Although the Course uses traditional Christian terminology, it is not a Christian doctrine. Its terms are used in a psychological context, with universal meaning for any student of spiritual principles, regardless of whether they have a Christian orientation.

Spiritual principles do not change, but we do. As we mature through the years, we access more deeply information we had only abstractly understood before. Twenty years ago, I saw the guidance of the Course as key to changing one's personal life; today, I see its guidance as key to changing the world. More than anything else, I see how deeply the two are connected.

That is why I have written this book. It is, once more and hopefully in a deeper way, my reflections on some of the principles in *A Course in Miracles*.

Looking back at *A Return to Love* several years after writing it, I was struck by the example I used of how hard it can be to try to forgive someone. I told a story about a man who stood me up for a date to the Olympics in Los Angeles and how I struggled to work through my anger and resentment. I'm incredulous now that I ever thought someone standing me up for a date was a profound example of the ego's cruelty. In the words of Bob Seger, "Wish I didn't know now what I didn't know then." It's pretty easy to espouse forgiveness when nobody's ever really hurt you too deeply.

Life was more innocent for all of us not so long ago. Today the world seems filled with such sorrow and danger; it's not so easy anymore to simply spout off metaphysical principles and expect everything to be okay by morning. These are times that challenge our spiritual assumptions, as the power of darkness seems to be taunting us, demanding, "So where's all that love you believe in *now?*"

The answer is that love is inside us, just waiting to be unleashed. The darkness is an invitation to light, calling forth the spirit in all of us. Every problem implies a question: Are you ready to embody what you say you believe? Can you reach within yourself for enough clarity, strength, forgiveness, serenity, love, patience, and faith to turn this around? That's the spiritual meaning of every situation: not what happens to us, but what we *do* with what happens to us and who we decide to become because of what happens to us. The only real failure is the failure to grow from what we go through.

The Challenge to Grow

Whether we like it or not, life today is different in ways we never expected. The speed of change today is faster than the human psyche seems able to handle, and it's increasingly difficult to reconcile the rhythms of our personal lives with the rapidity of a twenty-four-hour news cycle.

Dramatic endings and beginnings seem more prevalent than usual. Birth, death, divorce, relocation, aging, career change—not to mention the fact that the world itself seems so irrevocably altered—all seem to hail some kind of sea change. Things we thought stable and secure seem less so, and things we thought distant possibilities have come strangely close. Many people feel right now like we're jumping out of our skin. It's gone way past uncomfortable into a haunting sense that we might be living a lie.

It's not that our relationships lack integrity or our careers don't truly jive with our deepest soul purpose. It's deeper than that—some sense that reality is like a layer of cellophane separating us from a truly magical existence. We feel some loss of meaning like a sickness we can't shake. We would love to burst out, as though we've been crouching in a small box for a long time. We ache to spread our arms and legs and backs, to throw our heads back, to laugh with glee at the feel of sunshine on our faces. We can't remember when we last did that. Or when we did, it was like taking a vacation, visiting a tourist attraction. The most marvelous things about life don't seem to make up the fabric of our normal existence anymore. Or maybe they never did. We're not sure.

Most of us live with a deep, subconscious longing for another kind of world. We sing about it, write poetry about it, watch movies about it, create myths about it. We continue to imagine it though we never quite seem to find it. Our secret desire is to penetrate the veil between the world we live in and a world of something much more real. One thing we know for sure: *this* world can't be it.

Many of us are ready to make a break for freedom, to find that better world beyond the veil and no longer buy into the absurdity of a pain-laden world that takes itself so seriously. The question is, How do we do that? If the world we live in isn't as real as it's cracked up to be, and the world we want is on the other side of the veil, then where does that leave us?

Who among us doesn't feel displaced at times, in a world that's supposedly our home yet is so completely at odds with the love in our hearts? And how do we make the world more aligned with who we are, instead of always having to struggle to align ourselves with the world?

Perhaps we are living in a magic hour, like that between night and day. I think we stand between two historic ages, when a critical mass of the human race is trying to detach from its obedience to fear-based thought systems. We want to cross over to someplace new.

When we look at the innocence of children, as they love and learn, we wonder: So why can't people remain like that? Why must babies grow up to face fear and danger? Why can't we do what it takes to protect their innocence and love? You're not the only one feeling so concerned; the world is on a self-destructive course, and our children and their children's children are pleading with us to change things.

The times in which we live call for fundamental change, not merely incremental change. Millions of people feel called in their souls to the task of global transformation, wanting to be its agents in a monumental shift from a world of fear to a world of love. We can feel the time is now, and we know we're the ones to do it. The only problem is, we don't exactly know how.

How can we best participate in a task so huge and idealistic? We sense new energy rising up everywhere, calling us toward more enlightened ways of seeing, living, thinking, and being. Books arrayed in bookstores proclaim a better way to love, to lead, to live. Seminars and support groups keep us working on ways to improve ourselves, practicing spiritual disciplines and religious rituals. We get involved in causes and politics, licking envelopes, sending money. But somehow, still, we don't seem to be hitting the sweet spot, the miraculous key to turning the world around.

We can't avoid the news, the war, the terror alerts, the fear. We're doing what we can to change the world in our own small way, but new ideas and more compassionate forces seem over-whelmed by their opposites. A few things seem to be getting bet-ter, but many things seem to be getting much worse. Just when love seemed to be the hot new topic, hatred sounded its clarion call. And the entire world could not but hear.

The Eternal Compass

The most important thing to remember during times of great change is to fix our eyes anew on the things that don't change.

Eternal things become our compass during times of rapid transition, binding us emotionally to a steady and firm course. They remind us that we, as children of God, are still at the center of divine purpose in the world. They give us the strength to make positive changes, wisdom to endure negative changes, and the capacity to become people in whose presence the world moves toward healing. Perhaps we're alive during these fast-moving times in which "the center does not hold" in order to become the center that does. I've noticed in myself that if something small and ulti-mately meaningless has gone wrong—I can't find the file I left on top of my desk, my daughter failed to do what I asked her to do before going to a friend's house—I can easily get rattled. But if someone calls to inform me of a serious difficulty—someone has been in an accident, or a child is in trouble—I notice a profound stillness come over me as I focus on the problem.

In the former case, my temptation to become frantic does not attract solutions, but rather hinders them. There is nothing in my personal energy that invites help from others, nor do I have the clarity to think through what I need to do next. In the latter case, however, all of my energy goes toward a higher level of problem-solving: my heart is in service to others, and my mind is focused and clear. When I am at the effect of the problem, I become part of the problem. When I am centered within myself, I become part of the solution. And that phenomenon, multiplied many times over, is the force that will save the world.

When things in the world are troubling, our need is not to join in the chaos, but to cleave to the peace within.

The only way to gain power in a world that is moving too fast is to learn to slow down. And the only way to spread one's influence wide is to learn to go deep. The world we want for ourselves and our children will not emerge from electronic speed but rather from a spiritual stillness that takes root in our souls. Then, and only then, will we create a world that reflects the heart instead of shattering it.

The time is past for tweaking this or that external circumstance. No superficial change will fix things. What we need is more than behavioral change and more than psychological change; we need nothing less than for an otherworldly light to enter our hearts and make us whole. The answer lies not in the future or in another place. No change in time or space but rather a change in our perception holds the key to a world made new. And the new world is closer than we think. We find it when we settle deeply into the hidden, more loving dimensions of any moment, allowing life to be what it wants to be and letting ourselves be who we were created to be. In what *A Course in Miracles* calls a Holy Instant, we're delivered by love from the fear that grips the world.

Each of us is connected to a cosmic umbilical cord, receiving spiritual nourishment from God each moment. Yet in slavish dedication to the dictates of a fear-based ego, we resist the elixir of divine sustenance, preferring instead to drink the poison of the world. It's so amazing that we do this, given the extraordinary pain that underlies so much of daily living. Yet the mental confusion created by our dominant thought forms is so intense, and we are so trained by the world to do fear's bidding, that deliverance comes at most in flashes. Fortunately, there are more of those flashes than usual today. While darkness seems to be all around us, an understanding of a deeper nature is emerging to light our way.

That light—a kind of contemporary, secular star of Bethlehem—indicates newness on the horizon and beckons us to follow it to the birth of something fantastic. The wonders of the external world are as nothing compared to what's happening inside us. This is not an end time but a new beginning. What is being born is a new kind of human, played out dramatically in each of our lives. Freed from the limitations of the ego, free to see and hear and touch the magic we've been missing all our lives, we're becoming at last who we really are.

Toward the end of his life, the literary giant George Bernard Shaw was asked what person in history he would most like to have been. His response was that he would most like to have been the George Bernard Shaw he might have been and never became.

A New Beginning

It is an article of faith that God always has a plan. No matter what craziness humanity has fallen into, He has always delivered us ultimately to the peace that lies beyond.

Today, we can stand in the midst of the great illusions of the world and by our very presence dispel them. As we cross the bridge to a more loving orientation—as we learn the lessons of spiritual transformation and apply them in our personal lives—we will become agents of change on a tremendous scale. By learning the lessons of change, internally and externally, each of us can participate in the great collective process in which the people of the world, riding a wave of enlightened understanding, see the human race on a destructive course and turn it around in time.

To some this might feel like the period of a Great End, perhaps even at times an Armageddon, but in fact this is the time of a Great Beginning. It is time to die to who we used to be and to become instead who we are capable of being. That is the gift that awaits us now: the chance to become who we really are.

And that is the miracle: the gift of change.

CHAPTER ONE

Crossing the Bridge

Life as we knew it is passing away, and something new is emerging to take its place.

All of us are playing a part in a larger transformative process, as each of us is being forced to confront whatever it is we do, or even think, that keeps love at bay. For as we block love's power to change our own lives, we block its power to change the world.

Humanity is moving forward now, though in some ways we are doing so kicking and screaming. Nature seems to be saying to all of us, "Okay, it's time. No more playing around. Become the person you were meant to be."

We would like to, but it's hard. The problems of the world today seem larger than they have ever been before, making it easy to succumb to cynicism, fear, hopelessness, and despair. Until, that is, we remember who we are.

For who we really are is a power bigger than all our problems, both personal and collective. And when we have remembered who we are, our problems—which are literally nothing other than manifestations of our forgetfulness—will disappear.

Well *that* would be a miracle, you might say. And that is precisely the point.

THIS BOOK IS ABOUT LEARNING who we are, that we might become agents of miraculous change. As we release the fear-based thoughts we've been taught to think by a frightened and frightening world, we see God's truth revealed: that who we are at our core is love itself. And miracles occur naturally as expressions of love.*

It is said in Alcoholics Anonymous that every problem comes bearing its own solution. And the gift being borne by our current challenges is the opportunity to make a large leap forward in the actualization of our own potential. The only way the world can make a quantum leap, from conflict and fear to peace and love, is if that same quantum leap occurs within us. Then and only then will we become the men and women capable of solving the problems that plague us. As we leap into the zone of our most authentic selves, we enter a realm of infinite possibility.

Until we enter that zone, we are blocked, for God cannot do for us what He cannot do through us. To say He has the solutions to our problems is to say He has a plan for the changes each of us needs to go through in order to become the people *through whom* He can bring forth those solutions. The most important factor in determining what will happen in our world is what you decide to let happen within you. Every circumstance—no matter how painful—is a gauntlet thrown down by the universe, challenging us to become who we are capable of being. Our task, for our own sakes and for the sake of the entire world, is to do so.

Yet for us to become who we most deeply want to be, we must look at who we are now—even when what we see doesn't please us. This moment is driving us to face every issue we've ever avoided facing, compelling us to get to some rock-bottom, essential truth about ourselves whether we like what we see there or not.

*An asterisk indicates quoted material or concepts from *A Course in Miracles*.

And until we make that breakthrough in ourselves, there will be no fundamental breakthrough in the world. The world we see reflects the people we've become, and if we do not like what we see in the world, we must face what we don't like within ourselves. Having done so, we will move through our personal darkness to the light that lies beyond. We will embrace the light and extend the light.

And as we change, the world will change with us.

From Fear to Love

We spend so much time on unimportant things—things with no ultimate meaning—yet for reasons no one seems to fully understand, such nonessentials stand at the center of our worldly existence. They have no connection to our souls whatsoever, yet they have attached themselves to our material functioning. Like spiritual parasites, they eat away our life force and deny us our joy. The only way to rid ourselves of their pernicious effects is to walk away . . . not from things that need to get done, but from thoughts that need to die.

Crossing the bridge to a better world begins with crossing a bridge inside our minds, from the addictive mental patterns of fear and separation, to enlightened perceptions of unity and love. We're in the habit of thinking fearfully, and it takes spiritual discipline to turn that around in a world where love is more suspect than fear.

To achieve a miraculous experience of life, we must embrace a more spiritual perspective. Otherwise, we will die one day without ever having known the real joy of living. That joy emerges from the experience of our true being—when we detach from other people's projections onto us, when we allow ourselves permission to dream our greatest dreams, when we're willing to forgive ourselves and others, when we're willing to remember that we were born with one purpose: to love and be loved.

Anyone who looks at the state of the world today is aware that something radically new is called for—in who we are as a species and in our relationship to each other and our relationship to the earth itself. Yet the psychological fundamentals that hold this dysfunctional world in place are like sacred cows: we are afraid to touch them, for fear something bad will happen to us if we do. In fact, something bad will happen to us if we do *not*. It is time to change. It is time to do what we know in our hearts we were born to do.

We are here to participate in a glorious subversion of the world's dominant, fear-based thought forms.

There are only two core emotions: love and fear. And love is to fear as light is to darkness: in the presence of one, the other disappears. As we shift our perceptions from fear to love—sometimes in cases where it's not so hard and ultimately in cases where it takes spiritual mastery to do so—we become miracle workers in the truest sense. For when our minds are surrendered to love, they are surrendered to a higher power. And from that, all miracles follow.

Miracles

A miracle is a shift in perception from fear to love. It is a divine intercession from a thought system beyond our own, rearranging our perceptions and thus rearranging our world.*

The miracle is beyond what the mortal mind can understand. God's guidance doesn't come as a blueprint that the rational mind can follow, but rather as spiritual illumination, creating psychological breakthroughs that our mortal self could never achieve. And as each of us rises to our higher selves, we begin to reach each other at higher levels as well, combining our energies in more creative ways than we might have ever thought possible. Whatever is needed, our love will provide.

We will receive the "gifts of the Holy Spirit," arising to heightened dimensions of talent and intelligence. We will meet each other in magical ways. We will right the wrongs that had seemed unrightable. We will do these things through the miracles of God.

The moment the World Trade Centers fell, the complete solution to the problem that then confronted us was created full-blown within the Mind of God. The solution is a plan involving every human being, to the extent to which we make ourselves available to Him.

Everyone we meet, every situation we find ourselves in, represents a lesson that would teach us how to take our next step forward in the actualization of our selfhood. Everything that happens is part of a mysterious educational process in which we're subconsciously drawn to the people and situations that constitute our next assignment. With every lesson we're challenged to go deeper, become wiser and more loving. And whatever our next step is, the lesson awaits us wherever we are.

His work is the work of our greater becoming, and we don't have to be somewhere else, or doing something else, in order to do it. The journey to a better world isn't along a horizontal road but rather a vertical one; it's not a trip somewhere else, but only deeper into our hearts. Right in front of you, at this very moment, there are things to do and thoughts to think that would represent a higher "possible you" than the one you are manifesting now. In any given instant, there is more love we could see and more love we could express.

And as we do, we will heal the world.

Doing Our Part

As we change our perceptions, He will change who we are. When we have become who we are supposed to be, we will know what it is we're supposed to do. And when we have remembered Who is walking with us, we will have the courage to do it.

This book is a discussion of ten basic changes that each of us can make, from viewing the world through the eyes of fear to viewing it through the eyes of love. The predominance of fear-based thoughts has poisoned our psyches, creating a toxic meltdown within our minds. We seek in ways both healthy and unhealthy to escape into the sanctuary of a deeper truth. Yet it is not enough to just seek the truth or even to know the truth. We must give ourselves permission now to live the truth as we understand it, with all its myriad implications for our lives.

The miracle worker's task is this: to consider the possibility there might be another way.* There is. And He will show it to us.

You might be thinking judgmental thoughts about someone, and in this moment you could take a deep breath and pray for God to help you forgive them. You might be thinking about something you perceive to be lacking in your life, and you could choose to rethink that, concentrating instead on how much you do have. You might be worried about your ability to perform a job and then remember that God lives within you and there's nothing He cannot do. In any given moment, the greater life is available.

When we begin to *live* the greater life—not "seek" it, so much as simply *choose to participate in it*—then and only then do we find that it's all around us, all the time. God is in our mind. Wherever we go, He's there.

SOMETIMES THERE ARE ISSUES that we push to the back of a drawer, as it were. We know they belong to us and that we'll have to deal with them someday. But we keep putting them off and putting them off, and finally something happens to bring one of them to the fore. The universe makes it exceedingly clear: here, now, we're gonna deal with this one. Whatever part of our personality remains unhealed, it is time to heal it now. It might be a relationship issue, an addiction issue, a financial issue, something with our kids, or whatever. The form of the weakness is not what matters: What matters is that until we deal with it, we are limiting our availability for use in God's plan.

This is an all-hands-on-deck kind of moment on earth. It's not okay to be stuck in the smallness of our narcissism when our greatness is so needed. It is time for each of us to face once and for all whatever demons have kept us chained to our neuroses and pain; to stand up for our better selves as a way of standing up for God; and to take our places in God's plan for the salvation of the world.

This is an exciting time and a critical one. It's not a time to be a lone ranger. It is a time, despite whatever our pain or heartbreak, to reach deep into ourselves and humbly toward each other. For there we will find God, and in God there is every answer we are looking for, every solution we so desperately seek, and every joy we might have come to think was gone and gone forever. This is the time, and we are the ones.

And why are we not already functioning at a higher level of spiritual mastery? What holds many of us back is not spiritual ignorance but rather spiritual laziness. We *know* many of the principles of higher consciousness; we're just too mentally and emotionally undisciplined to apply them universally. We apply forgiveness where it's easy, faith where it seems to make rational sense, and love where it's convenient. We're serious, but not really. . . .

Now contrast that with the advocates of hate.

Do terrorists hate us just *some of the time?* Do they have a *casual commitment to their cause?* Do they take less than seriously the goal of full manifestation of *their* worldview? The only way we will triumph over hate is to become as deeply committed to love as some people are committed to hate, as deeply devoted to expressing our love as some people are devoted to expressing their hate, and as firm in our conviction that love is *our* mission as some are that hate is theirs.

A lot of us are already spiritual students; the problem is, we're "C" students. And that's what needs to change.

Living in the Light

Every moment we've deviated from our highest—bringing forth pain for ourselves and others—is a moment we deviated from love. It was a moment where we simply didn't know how to remain righteous and still get our needs met. We fall into ancient patterns of ego and fear, for no other reason than that we are subconsciously programmed to do so. And when all other efforts fail, we are likely, if only in the secret chamber of our heart, to ask God if He would please help us. And He will. He will reprogram us at the deepest levels. And then, through the alchemy of the divine curriculum, we'll meet the people we're supposed to meet, in order to go through the situations we need to go through, in order to learn the lessons that will transform us from beings of fear to beings of love. We will be given every opportunity to learn through joy, and when we deny ourselves that, we will learn through pain. But we will learn.

It isn't easy, giving birth to our spiritual potential. Spiritual labor can be very arduous—one holy instant at a time when we give it up, surrender, soften, don't care if we're right, forego our impatience, detach from the opinions and prizes of the world, and rest in the arms of God. But the end result is the love of our lives. We begin to feel more comfortable within ourselves, less laden by the chronic angst that marks the times in which we live. We begin to feel free at last of past hurts, able to fearlessly love again. We begin to exhibit the maturity and strength that were lacking in our personalities before. A new energy emanates from who we are, and others can see it too.

All of this is very simple, which is not to say it's easy. The spiritual path is not a matter of growing more metaphysically complicated; it's a process where we actually grow simpler and simpler, as we apply certain basic principles to everything we go through. We don't learn love, which is already etched on our hearts; we do, however, begin to unlearn fear.* And with every change we make from blame to blessing, we pierce the veil of illusion that separates us from the world we want.

Not every lesson will feel like fun while it's happening, and at times we will resist growth fiercely. But as long as we remain open to miracles—then we will forge ahead into a new realm of being, where love has erased the patterns of fear that have sabotaged us in the past, lifting us to unimaginable heights. Every situation comes bearing a gift: a chance to become who we really want to be and to live the lives we really want to live.

We will inhabit the world we choose to see, and that is why it is so important that we never lose sight of love. As we read about war, let's not forget the beauty of a sunset. When we think about the state of the world, let's not forget how many people fell in love today. God never loses His enthusiasm for life, and neither should we. Beneath the surface of worldly happenings, people continue to smile at each other and mean it, have babies, heal, create art, forgive each other, become more enlightened, laugh, grow wise, and love in spite of it all. In a world that seems split in two between fear and love, our greatest power lies in sharpening our own focus. Some things in the world today are very, very dark; what the world needs now is more people who are working for the light.

Seeing the light and then living in the light, we will ultimately become masters at the power it bestows.

Choosing a New Way

In the words of John Lennon, "You may say I'm a dreamer, but I'm not the only one." Dreamers must encourage each other today, as one of the ways our dreaming is suppressed is by making us think we're the only ones dreaming.

Suggesting anything close to the idea that love might actually be the Answer, we're swatted down like a fly by our contemporary thought police. We're told how naïve we are, how silly we're being, how unsophisticated our analysis of the world situation is. "She's a nut! She's New Age! He's a moonbeam!" Yeah, right. But those who build weapons systems to the tune of hundreds of billions of dollars a year and don't see a fundamental problem with that are *sane?* Those who propose building new and better nuclear bombs as the solution to global conflict are *sane?* Those who play with war like it's a little boy's new set of Legos are *sane?* The world has become like something out of Alice in Wonderland: the sane seem insane, and the insane seem sane. The entire world is completely upside down. But the good news is how many people know this; we've just been afraid to say it because we thought we were the only ones thinking it.

And we are not. A new commitment to love is rising up from the depths of our humanity, and its power is changing us on fundamental levels. Our mind has been opened to a liberating truth, and we feel this truth like an alchemical substance that bathes our cells and transforms our thinking. Though science couldn't necessarily register the change, we can feel that we're not the same. We have devoted our lives to a radical possibility: that love casts out all fear.

Externally, we don't really change. We still look the same; dress the same, play the game as the world defines it. But something has shifted in the way we see things. We sense another reality beyond the veil. The world we see is not deep enough to sustain us; we know that now and we stop pretending that it ever will be.* We are developing the eyes to see beyond the veil, and with that vision we will invoke a new world.

Every morning as we wake up, we can bless the world. We can pray to be servants today to something holy and true. We can take a deep breath and surrender ourselves to God's plan for our lives. And when we do, we will experience miracles.

What's most significant is this: *we are depressed if we do not*. For working miracles is the calling of our souls. We are literally dying to be born into the next stage of our spiritual development. The world's fear is old and dying away, and that's why it's so angry. Love has scarcely taken its first breath on this earth, and that's why it's so tender. But the meek shall inherit the earth for one reason only: their strength will literally take the place over.* Who we were is not as important as we thought, and who we're becoming is simply out of this world.

CHAPTER TWO

From *Forgetting Who We Are* to *Remembering Who We Are*

*T*o change our lives for the better, the first thing we have to do is stop projecting our ego-based sub-selves all over the place. Leading with Me the depressed, Me the insecure, Me the angry, and Me the frightened is not exactly the psychological equivalent of putting your best foot forward.

Yet these psychic splinters, as it were, are what we *do* lead with until they're subsumed into the grandeur of our true selves. Depression, insecurity, anger, and fear are not eradicated just because we have the right clothes, enough money, or the right credentials. They can be camouflaged, but only temporarily. People will almost telepathically pick up the truth of our deeper feelings and subconsciously reflect them back to us. All of us are involved in this constant interactive process, every moment, no matter what.

The only way we'll have *whole* lives is if we dwell within the *wholeness* of our true selves. And we are whole when we are one with God. The word *holy* refers to our connection to Him, and outside that connection we are dissociated from our own essence. Wouldn't it be weird to be one of Queen Elizabeth's children but somehow not know it? Wouldn't we be missing out on a pretty significant aspect of our identity? Magnify that geometrically in terms of psychological effect, and you have a sense of how bizarre it is that we've forgotten our Father is in heaven.

According to *A Course in Miracles*, what we have is an "authorship" problem.* Not recognizing our divine source, we express ourselves as creations of the world rather than as creations of spirit. The world has imprinted upon our psyches its brokenness and pain. And there is no point in trying to heal that pain until we heal our misplaced sense of heritage. We are not children of the world; we are children of God. We don't have to allow the false input of a weary world to affect us as it does.

Confusion about our divine heritage translates into confusion about ourselves: not understanding who we are or where we come from, we find it hard to understand who we are now or where we are now. And so we lack spiritual stability. In the absence of the sense of a divine creator, the mind assumes that we're our own creator and thus our own God. If God isn't the big cheese, then *I* must be the big cheese! And that thought—that we're it, we're the greatest—is not merely narcissism. It's a psychosis that permeates the human condition.

In remembering the truth of where we came from, we become more open to the truth of who we are.

The Great Awakening

In the Bible, it says Adam fell asleep—and nowhere does it say that he woke up.* It's as though the human race has been asleep for ages, not metaphorically but in a certain way literally. In our sleep, we have begun to dream. And some of our dreams have turned into nightmares.

Suffering is a nightmare. Addiction is a nightmare. Violence is a nightmare. Starvation is a nightmare. War is a nightmare. And the way we will change the world from being a place where these things happen to a place where they no longer do is not through what we *do* in a traditional sense, but because we wake up from the living nightmare in which they occur. We have been asleep without knowing it, taking part in a great forgetting—of who we are, what our power is, where we come from, and what we truly need.

But a great awakening is on the horizon, stirring like a new dawn in each of us. It's no accident that enlightened masters are called the "awakened ones." And now a species that has been asleep too long is on the verge of a mass awakening.

Resistance to this awakening, a lure to sleep, the false pleasures of numbness, are all real in our experience, but they are not as powerful as they appear to be. We are one with the Mind that thought us up, and nothing we make up separately has any meaning whatsoever.* When we remember we are one with our Source, we'll wake up to our power and our nightmares will disappear.

Ego versus Holiness

One of the exercises in the workbook of *A Course in Miracles* reads, "Love, which created me, is what I am." That statement amounts to a radical and counterintuitive evaluation of our true nature—for if I'm so good, then who is this person who keeps making mistakes, self-sabotaging, and repeating neurotic patterns?

That person is our fear-based ego. The word *ego* here means what it meant to the ancient Greeks: a small and separated self.

When we identify with the ego, it's like looking at a hangnail and thinking, "That's who I am." The ego is an impostor self, masquerading as who we really are yet in reality the embodiment of our own self-hatred. It is the power of our own minds turned against us, pretending to be our champion yet in reality undermining all our hopes and dreams. The ego is a delusional splinter that has cut itself off from our larger spiritual reality. It sets up a parallel mental kingdom in which it sees itself as different and special, always justified in keeping the rest of the world at bay. Seeing ourselves as separate, we subconsciously attract and interpret circumstances that seem to bear out that belief. That delusional kingdom is hell on earth.

When we remember who we are, when we stand firm in the light of our own true being as children of God, then the ego begins, however gradually, to recede. Darkness cannot stand when we truly embrace the light—when we consciously foster it and devote ourselves to it. That is why recognizing who we are—that we are love, that we are as God created us—is the most important thing we can do in any instant. Love is our spiritual reality, untarnished by anything that has happened in the material world.

When we forget this, thoughts of at least subtle attack and defense become a mental backdrop to our entire existence. The ego is "suspicious at best and vicious at worst."* And we should not underestimate its vengeance.* If we wish a genuine healing of our hearts—not just fixing things, not just bandaging the broken aorta of the spirit—we must question the ego's most fundamental assumptions. For only when we reject the ego's account of who we are, can we begin to discover who we *really* are.

And who we really are, is holy.

Our holiness is both the opposite of and the antidote to the ego. It is a state of being in which we have reconnected with our

Source, remembering that in fact we never left. We were created by God in a state of holiness, we were born onto the earth in a state of holiness, and we will return to this state upon our death. All of us, however, in between our infancy and death, fall asleep to our true nature and experience the hell of our self-imposed separation from God. Remembering our connection to our Source awakens us and frees us from the nightmares we create. In any Holy Instant, the ego is made null and void.

Holiness is not simply a theological construct, applicable to saints and enlightened masters but not to you and me. Keeping such a concept on a high altar, away from practical application, is simply an ego ploy to keep it at bay. To say that we are holy is not symbolic; it is to say that we are extensions of the Mind of God, and as such, our true nature is divine. When we stop to actually consider that we are children of God—not just children of this world—we begin to realize what spiritual wealth we have inherited. And it is ours to use, to cast out all darkness from ourselves and the world around us.

Through prayer we can work miracles in our lives. We have so much more power than we are using yet—to heal disease, repair relationships, reconcile nations, protect our cities, and transform our world. As long as we think that only "others" are holy, then only "others" will seem to carry miraculous authority. Yet it isn't true. In fact, all of us are holy, for all of us were created by God. As we open our hearts to Him, and to each other, our minds become conduits of the miraculous. Any and all of us can pray for miracles, and He hears any and all of us when we do.

When we have freed the inner resources of compassion that lie trapped within the maze of the ego mind, there will be an explosion of miracles that completely transforms our selves and our world. We will become reborn in spirit, free to express the creativity and passion that lie within us in a way that we never have before.

Few mortals have even scratched the surface of the potential genius we all possess and will one day realize. The great enlightened masters, from Buddha to Moses to Jesus, attained such alignment with spirit that the world around them was never again the same. They are elder brothers who demonstrated our potential. They showed us what each of us can one day become.

As the mind is permeated by the realization of the awesome power that lies within us, and as we allow ourselves to embrace the principles of higher awareness, the ego in time takes a backseat to higher truth. It cannot stand before a mind that has begun to awaken to its true reality. Eventually, accumulated spiritual knowledge pays off, and a larger life begins to emerge.

Infinite Possibilities

When I was young I didn't need a wristwatch, for at any time of day or night, you could ask me what time it was and I could tell you exactly. But something happened in my early twenties: it occurred to me that I should not be able to do that, and that it was weird that I could. And so, almost as soon as I thought that, I no longer could.

What happened to me is what happens to all of us: we are subtly and insidiously convinced that our natural powers do not exist. We become slaves to a worldview in which our human powers are diminished, seen as secondary to the astonishing powers of science, technology, and other false gods of the external planes. Modern progress seems to overrule our souls, leaving us bereft within a meaningless universe. There is no real God here, except the god of endless want.

We are trained, within this world, to see ourselves as the ego defines us. According to the ego's dictates, we are small and powerless, surrounded by an infinitely gargantuan and powerful universe. We are here but for a minute before we grow old and suffer and die. We are taught to identify with our guilt more than our innocence, and then we feel haunted by mistakes we feel will dominate the rest of our lives; we are taught to blame others more than to forgive them, and then we get stuck in feelings of victimization; we are taught that we are separate from others, and then we fall prey to grandiosity and insensitivity. We are taught that grades, credentials, past influences, mistakes, marriages, divorces, degrees, résumés, money, parents, children, or houses— whatever label or identity someone wants to stick onto us—are our essence. As a consequence, we forget who we really are.

This forgetfulness is the source of all evil, for it leaves us in personal darkness, confused about our heritage, our power, and our purpose. The mind cannot serve two masters, and when we forget the true one, we falsely bow before the other. When we mentally identify with the realm of the body, we see scarcity and death. When we mentally identify with the realm of the spirit, we see endless love, unlimited possibility, and the oneness of all things.

Look at the spokes on a bicycle wheel. At the rim, each spoke is separated from all the others. At the hub, each spoke is one with all the others. Each of us is like one of those spokes, connected with all others at the center, at our spiritual hub. Knowing ourselves as spirit is to know ourselves as one with each other, which is the esoteric meaning of the line in the Bible that "there is only one begotten Son." And that is why the Christ Mind, by whatever name we call it, is our salvation. It is a point of divine remembrance, saving us from the mistakes we make when we forget we are one with others. Spiritual renewal is the salvation of the world, because once we realize that what we do to others we are literally doing to ourselves, our thoughts and behavior simply change. To harm others, to refuse compassion, ultimately becomes unthinkable.

The Spiritual Basis of Self-Esteem

I have learned, when my life has been most painful, that the me who can be hurt is not the real me. The woman in me, the professional in me, the writer in me, the teacher in me—what do they all mean? Are they not but bricks in a spiritual prison, seeking to circumscribe my life, when in fact a life cannot be circumscribed? What difference does it make if someone betrays me when my real self, my spirit, cannot be betrayed? Is not an insult an opportunity for me to look at the part of myself that can be insulted and say, "Ha, you're not even really me"? Is not the true self beyond sickness? Then who is it that gets sick? Is not the true self unlimited? Then who is it that can be imprisoned? Is not the true self eternal? Then who is it that dies?

That is the question: who *are* we, really? For if we think we are only small and separate, mortal beings, then the world we create will reflect that belief. We will live in a world of separation and suffering and death. Yet when we change our sense of who we are—when we realize we are boundless, unified with all life—then the human experience as we know it transforms. The one exercise repeated in the workbook of *A Course in Miracles* states the following: "I am as God created me." In some essential way we still *are* who we were at the moment of our creation, and all problems derive from our forgetting that.

If you are as God created you, then no mistakes you've ever made or anyone's judgments or negative opinions about you can in any way determine who you are or change your value.* In the Holy Instant, we can remember our divine essence and choose to express it. And whatever we express will be reflected back to us. The universe is always ready to give us new beginnings that reflect our innocence, but we are not always ready to receive them. The sun can dawn, but we don't see it if the drapes are closed. No matter how much God loves us, we don't feel it if we don't believe it. As long as we think that we are less than God's perfect creation, then the experiences we attract to ourselves will be less than God's perfect creation. As we believe, so shall it seem to be.

Your value is inestimable because you are a child of God.* If you ever find yourself thinking, "I am such a loser. Time and time again I try, and I always fail," stop right there. Erase the tape by recording a new one. Say strongly to yourself, silently or verbally, "I'm the coolest person in the world because God creates only perfection. I recognize my inestimable value regardless of my mistakes, for which I ask forgiveness. I am God's creation, and in this moment I ask the universe to reflect back to me the greatness of God that is within me." (Let whoever needs to laugh at that, laugh. What kind of world are *they* creating?)

All the children of God are special, and none of the children of God are special.* You're not better than anyone else, but neither are you worse than anyone else. All of us have special gifts, all of us are born to shine in one way or another, and all of us are innocent in the eyes of God. Look at the children in kindergartens: they're all gorgeous and magnificent, and so are we.

It's not arrogant to believe that you're infinitely creative, brilliant, and potentially perfect through the grace of God. In fact, it would be arrogant to think otherwise because what God has created cannot possibly be less than perfect.* That fact applies to you and it applies to everyone. It is not arrogant, but humble, to accept God's gifts and allow them to be expressed through you.

Yet to the ego, that is not humility but arrogance, and you deserve a strong comeuppance for daring to believe in yourself.

Supporting Each Other's Greatness

We live in a world where judgments are made quickly and easily. Lies are told about people and printed by an irresponsible press; anyone can say whatever they want on their Web site and appear credible. People tear down others' reputations and assassinate people's character like it's a sport.

I've had a lot of judgment thrown my way since my public career began. For whatever reason—my womanhood, my convictions, my basic brashness—some have seemed to feel it was their duty to rain on my parade. Yet I've learned that you don't serve the world by taking on its judgments, hanging your head in shame, and saying, "Yeah, you must be right. I must be bad." Take responsibility for your part in your own disasters, yes—but take on every projection of guilt from every unhealed person? No! For whatever reason people may need to project their own anger and guilt on you, you don't have to accept it if it's not yours.

In some environments we receive basic support: "Go, girl! Fly!" And in others we get, "Who the hell do you think you are, trying to fly? Get down here, or we will force you down!" When we recognize the vengeance of the ego—how much it detests the spirit of life and love—we more easily avoid personalizing its vicious attacks. And there's learning in anything we go through. Both the challenge and the growth potential that comes from having had others judge you harshly is that it makes you have to decide for yourself what your self-esteem is based on: other people's estimation or God's.

The thinking of God is a hundred and eighty degrees away from the thinking of the world,* and one of the many areas where we have things completely upside down is in the area of arrogance and humility.* We never should apologize for seeking to actualize the greatness of God that lives in all of us. And those who refuse to support others in manifesting their dreams are only withholding support from themselves. Whatever I refuse to celebrate in your life, I will not be able to draw into mine. My thoughts about you are inseparable from my thoughts about myself. If I won't give you permission to shine, I can't give myself permission to shine either.

Today, living out our greatness takes on an urgency beyond fulfilling our individual dreams. Bringing forth our greatness is critical to the survival of the species; only if you get to live out your potential and I get to live out mine will the world be able to live out its own. Since limited thinking produces limited results, supporting others in believing in themselves helps to move the entire world forward. And becoming who we're capable of being—regardless of other people's opinions of us—is part of our responsibility both to ourselves and to God.

Unless we're supporting the emergence of greatness in the people around us, we're not doing our full part to help heal the world. A supportive smile, an e-mail, the smallest gesture can make the difference in helping another person believe in himself or herself. From a material perspective, what we give away we lose. But from a spiritual perspective, only what we give away do we get to keep.* When we're more generous with our support for others, the universe itself shows more support for us.

Surrender to Our Brighter Nature

Often we fail to develop an aspect of ourselves simply because no one modeled it for us. If a parent demonstrated "success" or "elegance," then we might have moved toward actualizing those things. But if no such model was present, either in the family or in the culture, then we simply didn't build the psychological track for that train. God, however, has built His own.

The psyche is like a giant computer with an infinite number of files. Imagine a folder called "God's Will," and inside that folder there are various files: Me the strong, Me the self-confident, Me the compassionate, Me the forgiving, etc. Everything that is God's Love is present as a file we are free to download. And none of God's files can be deleted.

Yet most of us have created some files that *should* be deleted. Me the arrogant, Me the sarcastic, Me the judgmental, and Me the cynical are all examples. They all belong in a folder called "Ego"; imagine Jesus sitting at your computer, highlighting that folder and hitting the "delete" key.

Me the angry or Me the arrogant is Nothing that has grown to seem like Something. It is part of the illusion of the world. It would be easy, however, to convince both ourselves and others that that is who we are, if we behave that way. And even if we *don't* act that way, as long as the negative file exists it acts like a seeping mental poison and has the capacity to hold us back.

Another set of imagery that reveals the truth of our eternal nature lies in fairy tales. The wicked stepmother is our Ego, and she wants to kill Snow White, who is the innocent spirit of love within us. She isn't able to, however, because what God created cannot be destroyed. What she *can* do is put Snow White into a deep sleep. It is only the kiss of the Prince—unconditional love—that awakens her.

If the prince had not kissed Snow White—if instead he had sniped at her, "What the hell are you doing, still sleeping!?!"— then she would not have awoken. It is not those who judge and condemn us, but rather those who bless and forgive us, who awaken us from our lower nature and return us to our better selves.

Someone once told me when my daughter was very little that it would always be best, when possible, to communicate with "Do this" rather than "Don't do that." I think that was some of the best parenting advice I ever received; you can see the damage done to people who are always being responded to in the negative. In their book called *Magical Parent/Magical Child*, Michael Mendozza and Joseph Chilton Pierce explain that the nature of the emotional bond between parent and child is more important than the specific information we impart to them. The tenor of our communication is as important as what we say. Our mission is to affirm the essential goodness in people even when they've made mistakes.*

I know that for me, someone constantly telling me I'm not okay is hardly what helps me improve. There is a magical power in relating to the good in people. I read in an interview where the actress Uma Thurman, daughter of renowned Buddhist philosopher Robert Thurman, said, "I guess I've surrendered to my brighter nature." She was taught well, I assume, that there *is* such a nature. The role of the parent is to see it in the child and reflect it back to her. And that nature exists in all of us.

That is a very different psychological approach to change than is normally associated with the Western mind. Usually, we think of our "negative" qualities as something we have to "get rid of." And from that comes all manner of dysfunctional parenting systems, educational systems, justice systems, etc. Imagine what the world would be if we looked at each other and thought, "I *know* there's something wonderful in there!"

In fact, our need is to *claim* and *cleave* to our spiritual potential, no matter whether it has yet been activated within our personality. That ultimate potential is our "Buddha nature" and the "Christ." To "accept Christ" is to accept that God's love is in us and in everyone. An eternal light is within us because God put it there, and invoking what we like is far more powerful than trying to destroy what we don't like. In the presence of our light, our darkness disappears.

Actors embody a character by finding its life force within their own. It is not so much another person, as it is another dimension of their own selfhood that the great actor inhabits. And most of us—whether we are actors or not—have dimensions of selfhood unexplored for no other reason than that we simply haven't chosen to explore them.

All of us can sing, though only a few of us are actually singers. All of us can paint, though only a few of us are actually painters. And all of us are actors, although usually we pretend we aren't.

In AA, it's said that it's easier to act yourself into a new way of thinking than it is to think yourself into a new way of acting. Just as children learn from playing, so do adults when we allow ourselves to. We vastly underestimate the ability of our subconscious mind to support us in creating change. "Fake it till you make it" is often good advice. When little girls play "house" or little boys play Spiderman, they are following a subconscious strategy of personality development, using their imaginations to prepare for new realms of being. And we need never stop doing this, unless we choose to.

Practice kindness, and you start to become kind. Practice discipline, and you start to become disciplined. Practice forgiveness, and you start to become forgiving. Practice charity, and you start to become charitable. Practice gentleness, and you start to become gentle.

It doesn't *matter* whether you're in the mood to be gracious to the bus driver today; do it anyway—and watch how it begins to affect your mood. Just push the button of the self you wish to be, and the file appears. It was already there, after all, just waiting to be downloaded. We become gracious when we *decide* to be gracious. We have the power to generate as well as react to feelings; to hone our personalities as we travel through life. In the words of George Eliot, "It is never too late to be what you might have been." It is never too late to become who we really are.

CHAPTER THREE

From *Negative Thinking* to *Positive Love*

A friend once told me that I'm a "sufferer." I didn't know what he meant, and at the same time I knew exactly what he meant. Things could be so good, and then I would find something really stupid to get upset about. I was simply in the emotional habit of focusing on the negative. I had yet to learn that to a very large extent, we are responsible for our own happiness. According to *A Course in Miracles,* happiness is a decision we must make. And who among us hasn't made decisions that were bound to make us suffer?

In any given moment, it's our focus that determines our emotional reality. There is rarely going to be a moment in your life when everything you look at, or think about, is absolutely perfect in your eyes. But perfection is a point of view; what becomes perfect is our ability to scan an environment and focus on it in the most helpful, loving, positive way.

There are always things to be happy about, and there are always things to be sad about. The bridge to a happier life is more an emotional decision than a change in circumstance. Life is like a piece of wet clay, and every thought we think gives it shape. A happy life can have sad days, but when you've mastered the fundamentals of a basically happy worldview, you attract more situations that prove your worldview correct.

And what could be a happier worldview than that love is real and nothing else exists?*

The trick, of course, is that it's hard to stay loving in a love-less world. And yet, with God, it's possible. When we spend more time working to view life through loving eyes, and less time try-ing to figure out why we're unhappy to begin with, then our lives transform much faster. The ego loves to foster the delusion that we're powerless before our suffering. For some people that is clearly true; but for most of us, that attitude is a self-defeating game we play, guaranteed to keep happiness at a distance, an always and forever "maybe someday."

Our capacity to change our minds is the greatest gift that God has given us, and it is also the most powerful.* He is present within us, in any moment, to help us return our minds to love.

We can always look at a situation and take a moment to focus on how blessed and grateful we are for the parts of it that are good. We can always invite the spirit of God to overshadow our thoughts, to lift them up to divine right order, to deliver us from the grip of the ego, and to turn us into who He would have us be. Every moment, we can invite Him to enter and purify our thoughts. And having done so, we will begin to see miracles. Some of them will seem small at first, but in time we will notice a basic shift in the tenor of our lives.

IT SEEMS TO ME THAT the key to happiness lies in getting over yourself. The happiest times of my life have been when I was more involved in something I was doing for others than in some-thing I was doing for myself. For any perception that focuses only on our separate needs will ultimately breed fear, and any perception that focuses on our oneness with others breeds peace. Many people struggle and fail to find peace within themselves because they don't really realize who their "self" is. That is why the ego is so dangerous: it would have us believe that we are separate, when in fact we're not. We can't have inner peace unless we feel complete within ourselves, and we can't feel complete outside our connection with other people.

You cannot find yourself by only looking to yourself, because in essence *that is not where you are*. The real you is an expanded self, literally one with the entire world. And so we find ourselves in relationship to the whole. We cannot be happy unless we are wishing everyone the same.

One day I was indulging some ego-based concerns about my life, worried that this or that wasn't happening; I remember I was specifically worried I wasn't achieving enough in my career. The conversation in my head was all about me (mistake number one) and focused on what I perceived to be lacking (mistake number two). I did realize my thinking wasn't miracle-minded, and finally I told myself to snap out of it.

I was packing to leave a hotel room at the time, and shortly afterwards the bellman arrived to retrieve my bags. I started asking him about his life. Questioning others about their lives rather than rambling on about our own is a surefire way to direct our minds away from the ego. I asked him what time he came to work each morning, what else he did with his life, and so on.

And then he said to me, "Excuse me, are you Marianne Williamson?" He proceeded to tell me that he and his wife used to attend my lectures regularly in Los Angeles, that his wife listens to my tapes every day, and about how important my work has been to them. And in so doing, he perfectly assuaged the concerns I had been focused on an hour before; his comments shifted my thinking and thus my feelings. But if I had simply stayed with my self-involved line of thought, without redirecting my mind to focus on another, then I would never have received the miracle. There would have been this person ready to offer me a healing, but I wouldn't have been available to receive it. By withholding friendship from the bellman, I would have been withholding healing from myself.

Generosity, in that sense, is an act of self-interest.* And I have seen it too many times to doubt it; as long as I remember that the love I seek can only be found as I extend my love to others, then peace comes fairly easily. It's when we forget that that all hell breaks loose. Love extended is the key to happiness; love withheld is the key to pain.

A Walk with God

I used to hear the old gospel song talking about a "closer walk with Thee," and I thought the image was sweet but quaint. Taking a walk with God is actually more than that, however, because metaphysically our "walk" means our line of thinking. To pray for a closer walk with God is to pray for help in thinking more spiritual thoughts, not because we want to be a religious goody-goody but because we don't want to sabotage our lives the way we did in the past. We are asking that our thoughts and actions be guided by God, now and always.

Being distant from God means thinking whatever we're thinking without any sacred touchstone for our perception. Since we've been trained by the thinking of the world, without God's guidance we are liable to reach instinctively for thoughts that are judgmental, blaming, or unforgiving. And thus we remain in the hell of separation from the experience of God's love.

A closer walk with God means narrowing the gap between our thoughts and God's thoughts. How many times have we done things we came later to regret, for no other reason than that at that particular moment we were not in touch with our higher selves? We were allowing a fear-based impostor self to pose as who we are, while our essential, loving self lay buried and bereft beneath the illusions of our unsatisfied lives.

The thinking of the world is like a computer virus that has invaded our system. The Holy Spirit is like an antivirus program that both protects us from false thinking and dismantles fear-based thoughts once they've entered our minds.

It takes mental discipline to retrain our minds, yet such retraining is imperative if we really want our lives to change. With every inspirational reading, time taken to meditate, or act of forgiveness or charity or love, we are shrinking the influence of fear in our lives. We can't change other people's thinking, but in fact we don't need to because all minds are joined.* All we have to do is change our *own* thinking, and as we do, the world will change with us.

We're not separate from God; we just think we are. What God creates is one with Him forever, as an idea cannot leave its source.* He is love, and He is All That Is.* Therefore, when we're not thinking with love, we're actually not thinking at all.* We're hallucinating.* And that's what this world is, in fact: a vast hallucination of the mortal mind.

We're separated from our own reality by a veil of illusion, and within that illusion we feel great fear. Imagine if God were holding your hand one moment, and the next moment you couldn't find Him. He seemed to have disappeared. Wouldn't feelings of panic set in immediately? Such is our despair.

All religions propose to cure our despair by lifting the veil of illusion. Some of them say it will lift after we die; others suggest it can be lifted while we are still on earth. From a miracle-minded perspective, the glory of God lies not just in what He will reveal to us later, but in what He can and will reveal to us now.

Let's say God has given you a tremendous gift—one you feel could be very helpful right now in the transformation of the world. Yet you don't have access to the people or circumstances that could pave the way for you to express that gift. God can arrange all kinds of things, but He will not determine your choices for you. If you do not choose to deal with the personal issues that keep you from expressing yourself at your highest, then you are choosing to block your own way. God Himself will bow before that choice, because the gift of Free Will was given to you at your creation. Yet He will move heaven and earth to help you choose again. He will find a way to offer you the chance to live a different life.

All thought extends itself into the world. If it was a thought of love, then more love is on its way out there and back around to us. If it was a thought of fear, then fear is on its way out and around, as well. We cannot interfere with what happens between Cause, which is the level of consciousness, and Effect, which is the level of the world.* God himself will not intervene between Cause and Effect, as the law was set up for our protection.* But we are always free to choose another thought, and *that* is our miracle. When cause with a little "c" (the thinking of the ego) is replaced with Cause with a big "C" (the Mind of God), the world of effects changes accordingly.

God has created the Holy Spirit as a "bridge of perception," from the outer realms of anxiety and despair to the inner realms of peace and joy.* And the Holy Spirit is always on the case, empowered by God Himself to deliver us from the ego's vain imaginings. Yet just knowing that He is there, and affirming Him with whatever name we choose, does not of itself bring us peace. That miracle occurs when we truly step back and let Him lead the way; when we disconnect from the worldly realms, if only for a moment, and sink into a place of radical availability. It's only when we are empty of—or at least unimpressed by—our own thoughts, that the Holy Spirit can fill us with His.

When we "come with empty hands unto our God,"* the Light of Truth shines away the ego, not all at once but gradually, with a cumulative effect. We become more open and forgiving, more vulnerable, and less defended—and not just with people we already know and feel safe with. If we're authentic only with people we already know, then we'll experience miracles only with people we already know! We can create a new beginning with everyone. If we allow Him to, the Holy Spirit will create a cosmic reset button, and from that point on we'll move forward with a different set of options—an *infinite* set of options. He rewires the world around us as we allow Him to rewire our souls.

There is a way of being in the world that transcends the world, a way of being regular people and miracle workers at the same time. We become the lamps that shed the light that emanates from the electricity of God. No one feels deeply at home on this plane; it is not where we come from, and it is not where we are ultimately headed.* It is a place we stay but for a little while, beautiful and blessed when we allow our perceptions of it to be overshadowed by His, but a way station nonetheless. We are here because we have a mission: to be the love that is missing in a loveless world and thus reclaim this darkened world for light.

Having and Being

We can *have* in life whatever we are willing to *be*. For ultimately, being and having are the same. When we grant ourselves the emotional permission to live the life we want, there is little in the world that can stop us. As it says in the Course, we don't ask God for too much, but rather we ask Him for too little.* Our weakness is often simply a weakness of faith—believing more in the limitations of the world than in the limitlessness of God.

To God, every moment is a new beginning. *And God is held back by nothing.* God would never say, "I could help you, but you messed up badly so I don't want to." Neither does He say, "I could give you a great life, but your parents were alcoholics so my hands are tied." Limitations do not stand before the limitlessness of God, and it is the limits to our faith, not the limits of our circumstances, that keep us from experiencing miracles. Every situation provides us the chance to live with broader, more audacious hope and faith that all things are possible. God is bigger than any limited circumstance in our past; God is bigger than any limitation that the world is showing us now. Limitations exist only as a challenge to us to mature spiritually, as we realize that through the grace of God we are bigger than they are.

Bigger than financial lack? Yes, because in God you are infinitely abundant. Bigger than sickness? Yes, because in God you are in total good health. Bigger than terrorism? Yes, because in God we are infinite love, and love is the one and only force that hate and fear cannot withstand. There is no order of difficulty in miracles.*

If enough of us pray each morning, asking the Spirit of God to enter into the global mess we've created and make all things right—surrendering our own ideas and asking for His instead—all things wrong will begin to dissolve. As it is, we're treating such problems primarily on the level of effect and hardly treating the causal level at all. Our faith in the power of the problem, and the power of human solutions, far exceeds our faith in miracles.

I once went to a meeting where the leader opened by saying that the task at hand was basically impossible but of course we would do our best. The group couldn't possibly move forward confidently once the leader himself had declared the job undoable. Yet had I suggested that everyone in the group simply take a deep breath, pause for a moment of silence, and affirm that the job could be accomplished effortlessly and brilliantly through the spirit within, I would have been viewed as a flake. The power of thought is like a great gold reserve always present among us, yet the ego's resistance to our mining it is rigorous and intense.

In both the Bible and *A Course in Miracles,* we are told that moving mountains is small compared to what we can do. Through the grace of God, we can heal the sick and raise the dead; we can work miracles in relationships whether personal, social, or political. The fact that at present we are not doing such things is not to say we are incapable of doing them. The fundamental issue is our entrenched resistance to even trying—indeed, even our anger at times toward those who dare!

Why are we more afraid of being powerful than of being powerless? What is it about the notion of God's unlimited power working through us that seems so threatening? Is it not in fact that the notion is an affront to the ego's authority?

Yet what, after all, has the ego given us? Is its material kingdom as powerful as it purports to be? Is its way really working, given the state of our planet today? Can enough consumer goods buy us happiness? Can enough sex buy us love? Can four hundred billion dollars a year in military expenditure buy us peace?

"My kingdom," said Jesus, "is not of this world." The problems of the world will not be solved on the level of consciousness which is the problem. Jesus also said, "Greater works than I do will you do." He did not say we do them now; he said we *will* do them. We will do them when we have evolved to the next stage of our spiritual maturity, a process that He, among others, will lead us to. Why, in a world that proclaims so much faith in God, are we so loath to let God show us how to move to the next level of our humanity? What is our resistance to the assumption of our own greatness as children of the Light? We are His beloved children, in whom He is already well pleased. If He created us perfect and has glorious plans for us in heaven, then why are we so intent on playing small while we're still on earth? Is God withholding His greatness until we die, or are we resisting His greatness while we yet live? The ego will say anything to keep us from God, and "You'll see Him *later*" is one of its favorites.

God is a blessing that permeates our entire being, everywhere and all the time. But it is not enough that God blesses us; we have to receive the blessing gracefully to experience it fully. How we receive something is as important as what we are receiving. If we accept a gift with genuine gratitude and humility, giving praise and honor to the giver, then our bounty will increase. When we simply take a gift for granted, however, not giving thanks, then our good will shrink. How many times have we casually minimized an opportunity, not recognizing some awesome gift of life and love until it was too late? We learned the hard way how much power we have to make things less, by simply thinking they are. Who among us has never thrown away a blessing, too cocky and spoiled, perhaps, to see it for what it was?

Countless days and nights have gone by in which I have failed to even notice the sun or moon. It's so easy to take for granted the glory that is all around us.

When I was a child growing up in Texas, I used to witness the extraordinary sunsets that Texas skies are famous for. I didn't know that not every sunset was painted like this, in manifold hues of pink and purple, orange and gold. I didn't know then that not every sunset displayed voluminous clouds and glorious rays of fading sun, dramatically painted across an endless sky. I didn't know how blessed I was to see this.

Sometimes now I miss those sunsets and realize how naive I was to think they were so easy to come by. I consider what miracles I'm underestimating now, happening all around me yet unacknowledged and unpraised. It seems to me the biggest crisis that faces us—certainly that faces me—is a crisis of faith. I forget that the God who paints those sunsets and keeps the sun in the sky and turns the embryo into a baby is active in my life as well. It is because of my own mental fatigue, the failure of my own imagination, that I fail sometimes to connect the dots between the problems that beset my life and God's infinite power to solve them.

One Problem, One Answer

All of us have problems at times, even serious ones. But while we think we have many different problems, we really have only one: our separation from God.* Once we're realigned with the Truth of our being, nontruth can't remain in our presence for long.

I told my daughter recently that life isn't about not having problems; it's about becoming someone who knows how to dwell within problems in a positive way. It's about taking full responsibility for however we might have contributed to a problem, forgiving ourselves and others, praying for all concerned, and developing faith that God's miracle is always on the way.

A problem isn't necessarily something bad; if it's happening, it's part of a divine curriculum designed as a learning opportunity for everyone involved. And one of the things we learn, when we have experienced problems and then received the miracle that solves them, is faith that miracles do happen. Miracles arise from conviction,* and nothing gives us conviction like having been saved from the bottom of our own deep hole.

Every challenge is an opportunity . . . for a miracle.

God can and will disentangle the myriad lines of dysfunctional energy that pervade a situation, as long as we place it in His hands. In your mind's eye, pour light on the troubling circumstance. Loosen your attitudinal grip. See it as a lesson—a potential display of God's miraculous power to heal all things—and surrender it with thanks to God. Feel your personal self no longer holding the problem nor having to solve it. Expand into the infinity of your being, and from there approach both the problem and its solution. In this way, you gain an added dimension of power to your ability to handle anything. We are heir to the rules of the world with which we identify.* Once we identify with spirit alone, there are no rules except those of mercy and love.

Dear God,
I lay this problem on your altar.
Please interpret this situation for me.

May I see only the love in others and in me.
Show me what I need to see,
Guide me to what I need to do.
Help me to forgive.
Raise me above the fear in my mind.
Thank you, God.
Amen.

The Power of Thought

It's easy to minimize the power of our thoughts, yet all thought creates form on some level.* You don't get karmic amnesty for, "Oh yeah, I thought that, but I didn't really mean it." The subconscious mind hears everything and simply reflects it back to us: there's no subconscious filter to leave out what we didn't really mean. Joke about how no one likes you, and pretty soon they probably won't. Affirm that you're in your power, and pretty soon you will be. The subconscious mind doesn't know how serious you are when you think something; it simply sets you up to fulfill your own expectations.

I loved the nerdy character in the movie *Love, Actually* who kept affirming he was a sex god and that women in America would adore him. His friend kept trying to tell him he was nuts, but he wouldn't believe it. And by the end of the movie he was in America being seduced by gorgeous women—several at a time!

Some people ridicule the notion that writing out fifty times, "I am smart and perform brilliantly at work," each night before you go to bed for thirty nights can be viewed as a serious agent of healing. Yet those same voices are often the first to argue that because your mother told you, "You're dumb and you'll never amount to anything," every night before you went to bed as a child you are wounded for life. So which is it? If words are dangerous, then words can also heal—at whatever age. Just as an audiotape can be erased by taping something else over it, we can begin to program our minds with thoughts that counter the ones we habitually think. For better or worse, the subconscious mind hears everything.

Remember, every thought we think takes us and others around us either straight to heaven (an awareness of our oneness) or straight to hell (the ego's state of separation). If we think good about the world, then we're liable to see it. And if we think bad, we're liable to see that too. We achieve so little because we have undisciplined minds.* We allow ourselves to wander far too easily into negative thoughts and negative words. And from both come negative experience.

Since all minds are joined, conflict between any two of us contributes to war, and reconciliation between any two of us takes us closer to world peace. Our smallest judgment adds to war, and our smallest forgiveness adds to peace. Miracles affect situations we will never even know about.* The butterfly's wings in South America affect the wind patterns at the North Pole, and thoughts of true peace in Idaho affect plans for peace in Palestine. What an extraordinary opportunity as well as responsibility we have, to try to get it right.

The Power of Language

One of the gifts we can give our children is to teach them the metaphysical power of words. "I hate school," "Everybody hates me," and "I'm not good-looking enough" are powerful statements that seem innocuous but are not. It behooves us as parents to teach our children that what we proclaim to be true will then *seem* to be true. At times I've caught myself saying negative things I don't even believe, giving in to a kind of mental self-indulgence that is the enemy of happiness. In fact, training our minds is as important as training our bodies and is just as important to our health.

Because of the work I do, I receive many letters from people around the world. There have been days when I was complaining or worrying about such meaningless things and then read a letter from a parent who had lost a child, a soldier's father asking for a prayer, or a patient battling cancer. My perspective was then radically and automatically altered. I have tried to develop the habit of gratitude and praise, as I realize how fortunate I am and affirm it with my thoughts. "Wow, what a beautiful day this is"—just a simple reminder of the beauty of life will literally make your life more beautiful.

The meaning of anything is the meaning we attach to it. I remember as a child that whenever I would complain about a rainy day, my mother would say, "Oh, no! The farmers need this rain!" What to me was a drag, to her was a relief.

A house looks so beautiful and you think if only you could live there, life would be so lovely; once you own it, however, there's the pressure of a mortgage to impinge upon all that loveliness. You think a purse isn't all that great, but then you see it on someone else and all of a sudden it looks fabulous. You think your husband isn't all that wonderful, but then someone else does, and all of a sudden he's fabulous. Everything we experience is filtered through our own thinking. How you see yourself is how you will tend to see your life, and how you see your life is how you will tend to see yourself.

I have known people who had so little and yet treated it so well. It's no surprise that what they had then increased. And I have known people who had so much and treated it so poorly. It's no wonder that what they had decreased. The world expands or contracts according to our participation in it. We are one hundred percent responsible for how we experience our experience.

I know a woman who has been through a terrible divorce and yet now glows from within. I once overheard her say, "You get bitter or better." I want to be like her in that sense; I want the negative to fall away, like a ball that has been thrown to me but that I don't have to hold onto. Even when we are victimized, we usually made some mistakes we need to take a good look at. And for that, we can thank even those who hurt us. For through the experiences they engendered, we will learn to avoid such situations. We will grow, and perhaps they will too. And life will go on, because God loves us all.

In God, there are no good guys and bad guys. There are loving choices which will be met with happiness, and unloving choices which will be met with pain. And the miracle worker interprets all that is not love as a call for love.* Regarded in this light, the closed heart of another cannot hurt us anymore. For it was not the closed heart of another that caused us to suffer but rather our instinct to close our heart in response. Pray for those who have wronged you, and the pain you have suffered will turn to peace.

It may not happen instantly, that is true. If someone lied about you, other people may believe the lies. If someone stole from you, it might take time to make your finances right. But that is the meaning of the symbolic three days between the crucifixion and the resurrection. It takes time for the light to ascend again, but it will. As long as our hearts are open while we're in the midst of a crucifixion—open to love, to forgiveness, and to what we ourselves need to learn and atone for—then resurrection is inevitable. Whatever it is, this too shall pass.

Radical Change

I've heard it said, "People don't change," but it is a principle of faith that through the radical alchemy of God's love, we can and do change. There is something in each of us that *wants* to become better, that *wants* to improve. The spirit is always seeking to rise up.

In 1999 one of my close friends adopted two young brothers, five and seven years old, from a county foster care program. Because they had been horribly abused by their parents, Carl and Dylan displayed common symptoms of severely traumatized children. As a consequence, they were not successful at transitioning into foster homes, much less an adoptive one. At one point they had even been on an adoption track with one couple and ultimately returned to the agency. They probably were on a slow track to the worst kind of life before my friend took them into his.

Many of the people around my friend, including me, worried that he had taken on too big a task. How could he, as a single man, cope with two traumatized young boys and successfully parent them? Yet as the weeks and months and years went by, all who knew them witnessed a miracle: little Carl and Dylan became model children, and no one who now meets them would ever guess that they came from troubled circumstances. My friend's love and radical care created the space for the boys to change. To grow. To become the children they were meant to be and still could be. Their adoptive father's patience and love accomplished an astonishing feat.

I read in the newspaper recently about a government study undertaken to determine what makes children learn. What was found—*after twenty-five million dollars of research*—was that the single largest determinant in making children learn is the presence of at least one adult—and this does not have to be a biological relative—who cares whether they do.

Miracles of personal transformation do occur, and they can occur in each of us.

Whenever our outer world remains stuck, it is incumbent upon us to look, not outward, but inward. It is a call to find the places in ourselves where we are holding on to old ways—where we blame others rather than taking personal responsibility for our woes; where we judge others instead of blessing them; where we are hard rather than vulnerable and open and kind. These issues hold the hidden keys to unlocking our unsolved personal mysteries. To achieve breakthroughs in the external world, we had best achieve internal ones. For the level of consciousness is the level of cause; addressing problems at their cause means addressing them inside our own selves. Addressing problems only on the level of their effects—in the outside world—is failing to address them deeply at all.

The Power of Love

When my sister was diagnosed with breast cancer in 1989, she said to her oncologist, "My sister says I should go to a spiritual support group." He responded, "And what medical school did your sister go to?"

The good news is that today such a patronizing, condescending attitude toward the physical benefits of spiritual practice is hard to find among doctors. If someone is diagnosed with a life-challenging disease, their doctor is now likely to be the first person to say, "Get over to one of those spiritual support groups." Why? Because the most prestigious academic institutions have scientifically substantiated that among people who have been diagnosed with a life-challenging illness, those who attend spiritual support groups live on average twice as long after diagnosis.

The fact we think love is a fierce and awesome power doesn't mean we're wimpy thinkers. I was once interviewed on a TV talk show, and the interviewer introduced me by making some snide comment about how I was a pacifist and thought there should be no army. I looked at him, stunned, and asked him where in the world he got that idea. "Well, I just assumed it!" he said. "You think love is the answer to everything, so I figured you think a military would be a bad thing!"

It's amazing how much ridicule the topic of love can attract when it does anything other than support the status quo. To go from "She thinks love is the answer" to "She thinks we shouldn't have a military" is to trivialize the most profound philosophical and spiritual truth ever expressed on earth.

A Course in Miracles says the world is an unhappy dream, which must become a happy dream before we can awaken from it.* That means the world must be transformed before it can be transcended. It is the *purpose* ascribed to something that determines its holiness, and there is nothing inherently unspiritual about the military. In fact, there are people at work within the U.S. military today who have more enlightened thoughts regarding future possibilities for our armed forces than one might think. Perhaps our military will manifest, in our lifetime, the ultimate fulfillment of the notion of "armed forces." They will be armed with psychological, spiritual, and emotional skills at building social and political relationships, as much as they are now armed with military hardware. Institutions evolve as consciousness evolves, and we are on the verge of a mass realization that if we want to change the world, we must become as sophisticated in the ways we wage peace as we are now sophisticated in the ways we wage war. Regardless of who ridicules us, it's important that we continue to celebrate love—not only the good feeling it brings, but also its actual power to heal all things.

On the level of true solution, love is the answer no matter what category of human experience. According to Mahatma Gandhi, love can heal all social and political as well as personal relationships. We've only scratched the surface of love's power, and when we dig deeply, we will find it to be more explosive than a nuclear bomb. We need an integrative approach to world affairs in which the emotional, psychological, and spiritual realms are given their place at the table of power. Jesus himself said, "Love your enemies, and pray for those who curse you." Martin Luther King Jr. said Mahatma Gandhi was the first person to take a love ethic and turn it into a broad-scale social force for good. And this is not just "nice"; it is imperative. King said we have come to the point where it is no longer a choice between violence and nonviolence; it is a choice between violence and nonexistence.

A few years ago, I was asked by Mrs. Coretta Scott King to speak in Atlanta at her late husband's official birthday celebration. I was one of the last speakers on the program. I sat and listened to speaker after speaker talk about Dr. King as though all he did was pour fairy dust over America. How great it was, all that l-o-o-v-e he spread! No one mentioned the fierce resistance he encountered, the struggle at the heart of his journey—a struggle for which he ultimately sacrificed his life. When it was my turn to speak, I had to mention that the love for which Dr. King both lived and died was not convenient to the status quo then and it is not convenient to the status quo now. Dr. King did not stand for sentimental love or popular love or convenient love. God's love is often none of these things. And if we are to truly honor Dr. King's memory, we must strive our best to do as he did—to take a stand for love even in the face of ridicule and hate.

The ego can destroy the body, but it cannot destroy an idea. The resurrection of both Gandhi and King lies in our willingness to stand strongly for the ideas that gave their lives meaning. Those ideas will give our lives meaning, as well. *A Course in Miracles* teaches that God is not looking for martyrs; He is looking for teachers.* Surely few among us have achieved a perfect love, an unconditional love. But the notion that a great wave of love will be the salvation of the human race is an idea whose time has come. And our willingness to be part of that wave gives a transcendent purpose to our lives. We are not naive about evil; we don't pour pink paint over it and pretend that it doesn't exist. We read the papers. We grieve the suffering. But many of us think God has a plan, and we believe—still—that its name is love. Not a silly love. Not a childish love. But a powerful love, an awesome love so aligned with God that it will change all things.

It will change all things, having changed us first.

Dr. King stressed the Gandhian concept that the end is inherent in the means: only if we try to practice peace can we truly be bringers of peace. And the universe will give us ample opportunity to try.

As I prepared to give my talk that day, I saw behind the podium a guest I had not known would be there: Mrs. Laura Bush. I had planned to speak about what Martin Luther King Jr. might have to say about President Bush's military policies, and all of a sudden I wasn't so sure about my prepared remarks!

I felt caught between a rock and a hard place. I didn't want to water down my remarks to make sure I offended no one. But I also didn't want to shame or embarrass the woman sitting near me by sharply criticizing the man she sleeps with every night. If I wasn't practicing sisterhood toward her, then I wasn't practicing peace.

I did a little editing of my speech, but not a lot. And every time I mentioned the president, I made some comment directed at Mrs. Bush about how our prayers were with her husband during this difficult time. I tried to express my disagreements with the president in a way that didn't personally dishonor him. At the end of my talk, I turned around to shake the hand of Mrs. King and then Mrs. Bush. When I got to the First Lady, I started to say I was sorry if I had sounded too hard on the president. But before I could say anything, Mrs. Bush put her finger to my lips and said, "Shhhhh . . . you did *great*." She was a generous woman to me that day. She recognized my effort to find a middle way, and I appreciated her acknowledging it.

Over and over again, in millions of subtle and not-so-subtle ways, people are bridging the divides between us. One day we will look around, and the divides will be gone—both those in ourselves and those in the world. We will have crossed over to a much better place.

Returning to Our Right Minds

We were born with a natural desire to extend ourselves in love, yet the thinking of the world then trains us to think unnaturally. Sometimes it takes something out of the ordinary to jolt us back to our true reality.

Once I had a terrible headache while flying, and by the time we landed I was feeling nauseated. I then got very sick, apparently with food poisoning. There I was, throwing up at a public stall in an airport bathroom, and all these women who had never seen me in their lives gathered round to help me. I could hardly believe it—they were putting damp compresses on my forehead, helping me get to a place to lie down, two of them even performing a powerful hands-on healing and prayer. I started to cry, and it wasn't because I was sick—I was crying because of how touched I was, having all these complete strangers take care of me.

I was reminded that day how good people really are. Another time, I choked on a peeled almond and couldn't catch my breath. My daughter saw I was struggling and exclaimed, "My mommy can't breathe!" The driver of the car we were in pulled to the side of the road, and several highway workers on the Detroit freeway gathered round me, one of them administering the Heimlich maneuver. Those men might have saved my life.

Such spontaneous compassion occurs when situations happen so quickly that ego thoughts of fear and separation are bypassed. Ironically, dangerous situations often bring out the *natural* in people. I have a feeling that the amazing ladies who gave me the hands-on healing in the airport that day might not have approved of some of my more inclusive religious beliefs; I'm not sure the highway workers and I would have related to our common humanity so profoundly in other situations. But in the moments when we are so purely alive—when we get to see, for whatever reason, that we are life and that life itself is so precious, we give ourselves permission to see that we are all brothers and to behave that way. That is what the world will be like when our minds have been purified and our hearts released to love.

What occurred, in those instances, is that everyone showed up instinctively to contribute what was theirs to contribute. And that is how the entire world can be healed—and will be healed—when we have been *returned to our right minds.* That is the problem with the world today: we are literally not in our right minds. At least in America, we have allowed a competitive ethos that is appropriate to our economic system to dominate our social interactions as well. We have in too many cases lost our sense of community connection and larger familial relationship as children of one God. Whether someone lives in a neighboring town or a neighboring country, they are our brothers, and all of us are equally precious in the eyes of God. We know that, but do we act that way? When we do, we will return to the garden. And not before.

All of us are on a spiritual path, but some people simply don't know it. All of us, individually and collectively, are being forced by circumstances to remember who we are in relationship to love itself. And we will learn this through wisdom, or we will learn it through pain. We can embrace the truth of our oneness, or we can resist the lesson and learn it later. But the longer we wait, the more chaos we will generate.

For the sake of our children, may we learn it now.

CHAPTER FOUR

From *Anxiety* to *Atonement*

I go back and forth sometimes between thinking the world is marvelously fine and then thinking it's completely screwed up.

And that, of course, is because both are true.

According to the Bible, after God created the world, He looked at it and saw that it was good.

"Oh, He did, huh? Well, that was *then*. It's not so good now!" I blurt out as I put down the newspaper with its reports of pain and horror.

"Your eyes aren't as good as you think they are." I look around to see who's talking to me. And I know who it is. I am talking to myself.

I look down at my finger, which I accidentally cut three days ago. I take off the bandage and marvel at how the cut has almost disappeared, the skin looking almost completely healed. I look out my window and see the first buds of spring on the trees outside. I notice the sun streaming through a stained-glass window in my kitchen. I live with the same sense of disconnect that most of us feel, between the glories of love and nature and the mess we have made of this world.

Every day I have two choices: I can face the day with this conundrum raging inside me, luring me toward anger and frustration. Or I can try to deal with this now, before I leave the house. I want to rise above the news reports, not because I didn't read them but because I understand them from a higher perspective. I don't want to be hooked into all the negative energy flying around today. But no mental concept can build the bridge for me, from fear to love and anxiety to peace.

I know myself. It's time to pray.

I go into my room, close the door, and light a candle that has a picture of Mother Mary on it. I start talking to her like she's my therapist. "I don't like what it does to my personality each time I read the paper," I say. "I don't want to be that way. I want to be more like you."

And then there is silence.

My breath begins to move more slowly, my eyes begin to close by themselves, and I relax into a place where I can feel her around me. It's not that she really says anything; she just takes me back to a natural place in my mind. I know that I am going home, to a world more peaceful than the world outside. And when I'm there, I know what my job is: to become this peace, to embody it fully, and then go back into the world and take it with me. That is what she would have me do. And this is what would heal my pain.

The House of God

Things are changing quickly in the world, and there's no sense we are headed in a more serene direction anytime soon. Getting on top of things at this time has less to do with mastering particular skills or gaining specific knowledge than with mastering our own ability to find serenity and quiet in the midst of raging storms. Otherwise, we'll be thrown off our game with every drama that the world has to offer.

The dramas of life are like weather patterns: inevitable changes within the course of nature. It makes as much sense to resist those dramas as it would make to resist the weather. Dress for them, yes; avoid the dangerous parts, of course. But try to control the dance of nature? I don't think so. When it rains, you simply go indoors. And so it is with God. When life is stormy, we can retreat into the House of God.

The House of God is a figure of speech that turns out to be much more than that. On the spiritual level, there *is* a house and it *is* our shelter. "May you dwell in the House of the Lord forever" is more than a symbolic statement. It means, may your perception of what's real and what's not real be based only on God's eternal realities, every moment. For if they are, you will be emotionally sheltered during the storms of life. People are born, we get sick, we die. We get rich, we get poor, we get married, we get divorced, we have children, our children grow up, we get new jobs, we lose old jobs, people bless us, some people betray us. And every change is a challenge to remember what's true. Love is the only absolute reality, which never changes and never dies. Dwelling in that which does not change, while things around us are changing all the time, is our key to inner peace.

When I was a child, people used to build bomb shelters—a now seemingly quaint effort to defend themselves in case of nuclear disaster. Our urge to go underground when things up on top have gone haywire is an instinctive response to the ever-changing forces of the outer world. And there is a corresponding spiritual truth. We need a shelter for the heart, and the House of God is that shelter where we can go every day to find peace.

We need that peace because the world is moving very fast now, and everyone's nervous system is affected by the sheer speed of things. Almost everyone seems frazzled, like we need a vacation to get back to ourselves, a few days just lying on a beach to restore our natural balance.

We pretend the speed doesn't affect our children, but we suspect it does. We allow them to sit for hours in front of television and computer screens at such an early age that their brains would have to be affected. I saw a note written by a ten-year-old: "I'm a total f–ing nervous wreck." We clearly have a problem here.

Yet the children are simply mimicking us. We're all running so fast we can't possibly be thinking at our best or feeling our best. The mind and the body need empty space if the voice for God is ever to break through. And yet, even though we're frantic, I think we're addicted to the adrenaline of our modern lives. We keep moving as a way of not dealing with something. If we move fast enough, perhaps we'll all just forget how much we hurt.

Our existential pain becomes impacted, pushed down, and then it eats away at us from the inside. As we age, we start developing physical symptoms of early breakdown. The body can carry just so much stress before it acts like Yertle the Turtle at the bottom of the heap and cries out, "No more, no more!" Physical crisis, emotional crisis, family crisis, whatever it is . . . nature takes so much, and then it blows. Then we have the financial and every other kind of pressure that goes along with dealing with all the crises created because we had so much pressure to begin with.

If we want to, we can stop this. In God, there is a way.

The Stress of a Contracted Heart

In every moment, we either expand the heart or contract it.

When the heart is contracted, other things become contracted as well: your relationships, your career, your money, your health, your life.

We often contract as a response to stress, as though we're trying to defend against an oncoming force. But in fact, if I contract to avoid pressure, I inevitably create more of it. Why? Because my behavior when I'm contracted—tough, stressed, angry—then causes situations that add more stress.

The antidote to stress is counterintuitively to relax into it. If you have kids to raise, a job to complete, a paper to write, and two business trips to take before the end of next week, you will help yourself not by tensing up but by loosening up. Your contracting won't somehow help it all come together in time. Quite the opposite: loosen up, and time will loosen up as well. According to Einstein, time and space are illusions of consciousness. Like everything else, they take their lead from you.

Recognizing the origins of stress from a spiritual perspective, we find a key to dismantling the thoughts that produce it. Stress is simply the inevitable consequence of thinking the unreal is real. In that sense, stress is a choice.

If an issue is "of the world," then attaching to it our sense of success or failure, satisfaction or lack of satisfaction, is a setup. Nothing in the world can give us a deeper peace because the spirit is not at home in the world. To the extent that our sense of well-being is tied in any way to the things of the material world, we will be prone to worry and anxiety.

Yet we almost feel we *have* to stress when there's so much to do, so much that can happen, so much to consider all the time!

That, however, is the joke: the only reason things seem to press upon us so heavily is because we think they are so heavy.

If we ourselves had to hold all the balls in the air that we feel we're juggling all the time, then we would have every reason to feel depressed and scared. But the fact is, we're only juggling them because we think we need to—and because we think we need to, we do! Once we realize we have a choice—that the universe is as tight or as loose as we perceive it to be, that time is as limited or expanded as we perceive it to be, that things are as difficult or as easy as we perceive them to be—then stress begins to evaporate. We literally "lighten up." Every time we think, "Oh, my God, I have so much to do and I don't know how I can do it," we can change our thinking. We can place all our burdens in the hands of God, ask for a miracle, and thank Him in advance for providing it. We will stop being so tense; we will stop being so worried; we will stop living a life so devoid of joy. The lying ego will say things like, "I can't do that! I have responsibilities!" Yet that's exactly the point: once we've lightened up, we attract the people and circumstances that provide us the means to effortless accomplish a task. It's not like working miracles *isn't doing anything.*

Why are we so worried, after all, if miracles lie at our fingertips? Our very being is a space for miracles, and whatever our problem is, we can release it into the hands of God. To pray "God, please take this" is an act of empowerment, not weakness. Who in their right mind wouldn't choose miracles over stress if they truly knew they had a choice?

Sometimes people talk about the "committee" in their head, the endless chattering of the ego naysaying them throughout their day. I've learned something about that committee in my head: I've learned it's up to me to take charge of the meeting. It's up to me to think positive thoughts so there's no room for all the negative ones. When I use a miracle-minded "problem-solving repertoire"*—looking for eternal rather than worldly insight, standing in faith and asking for miracles—I stop living at the effect of worldly drama. It's my responsibility to remind myself how blessed I am and to extend that blessing to others. When I remember that God's power is unlimited, I stop stressing about how limited mine is.

It's all up to me, because it's all inside my head.

One night I was having a particularly hard time enduring one of those stretches of desperate hours that are the meaning of a spiritual wilderness. Too many things had piled up, any one of which I probably could have handled okay but the combination of which had sent me reeling. A large theft, betrayal by people I thought were honorable—a few things like that and I was reeling. It was almost five in the morning, and I hadn't been able to sleep, though I couldn't work, read, or do much of anything else either. All I could do was catalog my perceived disasters, and I remember actually saying out loud, "Dear God, I feel like such a failure."

Five minutes later I picked up a Fed Ex package sitting next to my bed. It had arrived the day before, containing the galleys of Rabbi Harold Kushner's new book. He had asked me to read it, and I figured I would get to it when I could. I picked it up in an effort to get out of myself, to do something for someone else, to try to counter the spiral of self-pity that was taking me down such a dark and painful hole.

As I began the book, my jaw dropped open. I felt I was encountering the words of God. Kushner wrote that feelings of failure occur in all our lives, and the issue is who we become as a result. Reading his words that morning, I was given the ability to completely recontextualize my experience, reframe my feelings, and grab onto some hope. The book provided a sense of transcendent meaning for my sorrow, leaving me not only able to finally fall asleep but also to wake up later with energy and enthusiasm.

I couldn't believe that that particular book, with that particular theme, just happened to be sitting next to my bed at that moment. And it wasn't lost on me that Harold is a rabbi, bringing me comfort from my own religious tradition. I knew that the shift in perception his words introduced into my mind was truly a miracle. It was not a change in what had happened to me; it was *a different way to think about* what had happened to me. God—and Rabbi Kushner—had graced me with a different point of view.

Comfort Comes

A few weeks before my father died, he was lying on his favorite bench, already gravely ill, and I was sitting on the floor next to him. He had an intense but faraway look in his eyes, and he said, "I'm not afraid. I know where I'm going." I simply looked at him and shared the moment, but I've often wished since that I had asked for more explanation. He clearly perceived an eternal reality that would carry him through death.

It shouldn't have to take death to make us so much more aware of what matters and what doesn't, what's eternal and what's not. Why can't we remember much, much sooner that love is all that matters and love is all that lasts? It's as though, when death is at the door, we're given a free dose of sacred understanding. Perhaps if we asked for it earlier, it would come.

> Dear God,
> May the Holy Spirit overshadow my mind,

And give me eyes to see.
May I perceive the love I know exists
And overlook the rest.
May I rise above the darkness of the world
and my mind be bathed in light.
May I be calm and comforted
By Truth.
Amen.

Digging Deep

Underneath the layer of our normal thinking lies a level of consciousness that is pure love and peace. Yet we cannot reach that consciousness simply by deciding to; we have to dig deep into the ground of our inner being, creating a space of listening for the "small still voice for God." The more things are happening on the outside, the more important it is to find that stillness on the inside.

Every mistake we ever made occurred because, in the moment we made it, we were not in conscious contact with our highest self. We were not centered in our spirit. That is why making that contact, and spending time each day fostering it, is the single most powerful thing we can do.

How many times have we made a mistake that affected the rest of our life simply because at the moment we made it we were moving too fast, at the effect of our stress or anger or fear? Would we have made that mistake had we remembered in that moment who we really are in a spiritual sense and who others are in relation to us? At the mercy of negative, shallow thoughts, we are bound to misperceive ourselves and others.

What happens in life depends on who we are in life. What we experience throughout the day has everything to do with who we are throughout the day. And who I am during the day has a lot to do with how I start it.

Five minutes spent with the Holy Spirit in the morning guarantees He will be in charge of our thought system throughout the day.* In every single moment, we choose between love and fear, yet the ego speaks first and the ego speaks loudest. The voice for God will not impose itself; it has to be received, made space for, and welcomed into our minds. When we reach out to God and welcome His comfort at the beginning of the day, then something happens. It's not that we become perfect, but we become more aware. And that awareness makes us miracle-ready in a way we would not otherwise be.

Every morning when I wake up, I try to remember to give praise and thanks. Thank you, God, for my life today. Thank you for my family and friends, thank you for my home, thank you for my many blessings. Thank you for Your healing power, now pouring forth upon me. I claim it now, and pray for miracles. Please bless this day, for me and everyone. Amen.

Meditation

In addition to prayer, we need quiet time with God. And that is the purpose of meditation. Meditation is like soaking a dirty pot in soapy water. Sometimes food gets stuck on the surface of a pot and the only way to clean it is to let it soak overnight. Through soaking, the dried food softens and finally rises to the surface. Quiet time with God is like a spiritual soak in which fearful thoughts that are clinging to the surface of the mind are loosened and then finally rise and depart.

Notice there's a time when the food begins to rise and the water gets dirtier, not cleaner. So it is that during meditation we might feel more agitated before we feel more peaceful. But feeling agitated is just a point in the process, to be endured until it passes.

Unless we take the time to meditate—to allow the alchemy of the Holy Spirit to transform the deepest regions of our mind— we carry fear-based, guilt-ridden thoughts around like a spiritual weight around our necks. We usually experience the effects of these thoughts as free-floating anxiety, not even sure what it is that's causing us to be nervous and depressed. Guilt and blame have permeated our thinking, causing constant discomfort and emotional chaos. Meditation is the only way to address, and eradicate, the deeper layers of our angst.

We might be walking down the most beautiful street on a gorgeous spring day, enjoying a day out with someone we love. But we won't be happy if upsetting thoughts continue to distract us. Life isn't a television commercial where if everything *looks* good then it must *be* good. You can buy the product they're selling and try to change the picture. But you can also meditate for free and change your life.

One hurried day, I had just enough time to take a quick glance into the *Course in Miracles* workbook before I left the house. I read the sentence, "My holiness envelops everything I see." As I went about my day—sitting in a cab, ordering a soy latte, waiting for an elevator—I said the sentence to myself whenever I could. I felt my sense of nervousness abate as I did so, and I wanted to kick myself for not having taken at least five minutes alone to do the exercise before leaving the house that morning. I'd had reasons, of course—I was late for a meeting, and so on. But I knew in my heart that I'd had more than reasons; I'd had resistance. As clear as I am that meditation will radically alter my day, it's amazing to me how often I still avoid it. Not like I used to, but every once in a while. And who wants their life to be less than it could be *every once in a while?*

The Indian gurus are right who say that no matter what the problem, the answer is to meditate. They're right because, as Einstein said, we won't solve the problems of the world from the level of thinking we were at when we created them. Meditation changes the level of our thinking, and that's why it changes our lives.

Particularly today, each of us carries more worry and upset than we realize. It bombards us even from halfway across the world. Much that we thought we could count on we suddenly discovered we can't count on at all. The September 11 attacks on the United States have been like a time-release capsule of collective anxiety. In a day, everything changed, and we're being forced to learn a deeply spiritual lesson: that the only real security lies in our internal strength. Anything can happen to anyone at any time. Yet our disillusionment simply means we were laboring under an illusion before—thinking external safety could be guaranteed. Now that we know which houses were built on sand, we have the opportunity to rebuild them on rock. Every time we meditate, it's like we're creating a secure underground location where we can retreat when times are rough.

In his book *The Soul's Awakening,* philosopher Rudolf Steiner wrote, "He who would create the new must be able to endure the passing of the old in full tranquillity."

When we meditate in the morning, we are placing our minds, emotions, and nervous systems at God's service. We are choosing not to be merely a jumble of nerves, stress, frantic efforts, vain imaginings, and fear, walking around in a body and pretending to be a person. The poet Lord Byron once wrote of his age, "We are living in gigantic and exaggerated times." And so are we. A huge drama is being played out on the earth today, and we're choosing to be part of it. We are signing up for prophetic duty. We are asking to be used for an effort much bigger than ourselves. We realize that the emergence of wiser, stronger, more intelligent and compassionate people is the single most important factor in the salvation of the world—and that is what we want to be. But it's hard to be any of those things if we're jumping off the walls.

Many times at my lectures I've heard a question that goes something like this: "I try so hard, but I just can't find the peace of God. Can you help me?"

I respond, "Do you do a serious prayer and meditation practice every day?"

"No," they say.

"Funny," I say. "I knew that."

Spending Time with God

The Holy Spirit responds fully to our slightest invitation.* The problem isn't that the Holy Spirit doesn't respond, the problem is how deep we sink into a problem before we bother to ask for His help. We have this ridiculous, self-defeating habit of going to God as a last resort instead of making Him our first call.

That's why constant spiritual practice matters. It takes at least a daily reminder to remember to put God first. The ego is sly and insidious; in the words of Sigmund Freud, "Intelligence will be used in the service of the neurosis." If you think you're too smart to have to worry about your ego, you have to worry about it even more.

If we meditate sometimes but not always, then it will seem to us that God helps us sometimes but not always. If we pray and meditate on some days but not all days, then we will feel the peace of God on some days but not all days. If we go to God only when we're in trouble, then of course His help seems inconsistent. Yet the inconsistency lies in us. The more time we spend with God, the more we develop our spiritual musculature and the stronger we become in dealing with life's challenges. I remember the song lyric, "Darlin', if you want me to be closer to you, get closer to me." The same applies to our relationship with God.

The form of your practice doesn't matter. It might be the workbook of *A Course in Miracles*, transcendental meditation, or Buddhist or Jewish or Christian meditation. What matters is that you practice.

Meditation rests the mind the way sleep rests the body. In Zen Buddhism there is the concept of "no mind" or "beginner's mind"; in the I Ching it is said that our mind should be like an empty rice bowl. In *A Course in Miracles* it is stated, "Forget your ideas of good and bad, forget your ideas of right or wrong, forget this Course, and come with empty hands unto your God." The idea of emptying one's mind is fundamental to all meditative practice. For once we have surrendered our extraneous thinking, then God's truth can move into the vacuum. We substitute His Mind for our mind, and thus they become one.

Five minutes in the morning is better than nothing. Thirty minutes provides serious spiritual support. Not meditating at all? Expect the stress to continue.

You can make another choice: close your eyes, breathe in the quiet, surrender it all . . .

This is from the workbook of *A Course in Miracles:*

Five minutes now becomes the least we give to preparation for a day in which salvation is the only goal we have. Ten would be better; fifteen better still. And as distraction ceases to arise to turn us from our purpose, we will find that half an hour is too short a time to spend with God.

Each hour adds to our increasing peace, as we remember to be faithful to the Will we share with God. At times, perhaps, a minute, even less, will be the most that we can offer as the hour strikes. Sometimes we will forget. At other times the business of the world will close on us, and we will be unable to withdraw a little while, and turn our thoughts to God.

. . . And we will quietly sit by and wait on Him and listen to His Voice, and learn what He would have us do the hour that is yet to come; while thanking Him for all the gifts He gave us in the one gone by.

In time, with practice, you will never cease to think of Him, and hear His loving Voice guiding your footsteps into quiet ways, where you will walk in true defenselessness. For you will know that Heaven goes with you. Nor would you keep your mind away from Him a moment. . . .

Your practicing will now begin to take the earnestness of love, to help you keep your mind from wandering from its intent. Be not afraid nor timid. There can be no doubt that you will reach your final goal.*

If You Do It, It Works

Intellectually understanding spiritual principles doesn't guarantee enlightenment, and the ego loves to use religion and spirituality as a cover.

One moment of enlightened awareness doesn't completely transform your life. The spiritual path is slow and arduous at times, as every single circumstance becomes the ground on which both ego and spirit seek to make their stand. Spiritual practice is like physical exercise: it has a cumulative effect, and if we want to enjoy its benefits, we can never stop doing it. You can't just go to the gym once and walk out with a new body, and neither can you attend one seminar, say one prayer, or sing one hallelujah and expect your life to be perfect from now on.

The mind as well as the body demands training if it's to perform at full capacity. That's why some of us go to the gym or do yoga regularly and also why we participate in religious services or spiritual practice regularly. In a world where thoughts based on fear prevail, you're going against the flow to make a true and genuine stand for love. It's not easy to walk up two flights of stairs when you're not in physical shape, and it's not easy to make an unpopular stand for faith and forgiveness when you're not in spiritual shape.

Yet if we're going to make the change from the world that is to the world that could be, it's exactly that stand that is necessary. There's nothing spiritual about avoiding the problems of the world. Our goal is not to *avoid* the world, but to heal it. Yet we can't give to the world what we ourselves don't already have; the gifts of the spirit can only be given by those who are trying to embody them. That's why, as Gandhi said, we must *be* the change we want to see happen in the world. Peace has to begin in our own lives and spread outward to heal others as we interact with them in a loving way.

The Atonement

The Atonement is the crux of spiritual practice; it is the corrective process by which our thoughts are moved by the Holy Spirit from where they have been to where they should be. But He can't enter where He's not invited, as that would be a violation of our free will. He cannot take from us what we haven't released to Him.*

To atone, we have to be willing to take an honest look at the thoughts we thought and the things we did whether or not they're fun to look at. We have to be willing to cringe, to admit where we were wrong in a thought, an action, or a word. The reason we "atone" to God rather than ask His forgiveness is because God has never judged us. We atone not because God is angry but because even He will not violate His law of Cause and Effect.

Martin Luther King Jr. used to say that while the nonviolent movement was materially passive, it was spiritually active. Since the level of consciousness is the true level of cause, then you can sometimes do more to move a mountain from sitting in your armchair than from running around the mountain or even climbing it. What we move on the level of consciousness is moved within the Mind of God.

Atonement is God's greatest gift, allowing us to get back on track when we've gotten off. Practiced by Catholics in confession and Jews on the Day of Atonement (Yom Kippur), Atonement for our sins is the act that reconciles the Creator and the created. It takes work to take full responsibility for the mistakes we've made, atone for them, and try to make things right. But it is the work God would have us do.

"The primary responsibility of the miracle worker is to accept the Atonement for himself."* The Atonement is first and foremost a correction in our thinking, a prayerful return to the love in our hearts. Then we may or may not need to take direct action; if there's something for us to do, He'll let us know.*

When we have made a mistake, the universe records it. But God would have us atone for our errors, not suffer for them. We are asked in whatever way is appropriate and possible to make amends for our wrong-minded behavior. God has sent the Holy Spirit to correct us when we need correction, and through the Atonement He provides us with the chance to begin again, no matter how far we've strayed from the truth in our hearts. Our ability to begin anew is supported by God Himself, as long as we approach Him with a contrite and humble heart. Nothing in our past diminishes the infinite possibilities inherent in our present as long as we atone for our errors and return to love.

Conscience is important, as is remorse. But they are meant to lead us to new life, not leave us drowning in a sea of guilt. When we have chosen fear instead of love—and who among us hasn't?—then the love we might have chosen "is held in trust for us by the Holy Spirit" until we are ready to receive it.* To me, that's one of the most incredible principles in *A Course in Miracles.* It's amazing when you think about it: I could have said or done the right, loving thing, and if I had, then such and such a thing would then have happened. However, I did not. I've been trained by the world to think with fear, and I did. *Yet God saved the possibility I turned down, until I'm ready to return to love and choose again!*

How much love and mercy has to be built into the structure of the universe for this to be so! As long as we atone for a mistake, we will be given the chance to correct it. That chance might not come in the form we would wish, but it will be there in a form that God determines.

One day I heard about a woman I had known many years earlier. She had suddenly stopped speaking to me, and I didn't know why.

Then I thought about it, and I did know why.

I had made a comment about her that had probably reached her ears. It wasn't a vicious or cruel comment, but it wasn't gracious either. I'd put it in the category of unconscious and unkind.

So here it was, over ten years later, and she had just done something really wonderful. I wanted to acknowledge her, and I also wanted to tell her how sorry I was for having made such a wrong-minded comment all those years earlier and ask her to forgive me. I didn't know her address or whether or not she would read my letter. But in my heart I atoned. I really got that I had been less than the person I should have been, and I was eager to make amends.

The very next day I was called by a reporter for a major European newspaper. They were writing an article about her, and they asked my opinion. I had the opportunity to go on and on about how wonderful she is, what good things she's done—in a venue where I could be fairly certain it would reach her eyes. Synchronicity is the handwriting of God: as soon as I atoned, the entire universe was programmed to catch up to my corrected perception.

When our thinking is corrected, then so is our world. We're punished not *for* our sins but *by* our sins. *And through prayer, they are transformed.*

"Prayer is the medium of miracles. . . . Through prayer love is received, and through miracles love is expressed."* If you want a miracle in your life, simply pray for one. For as long as you are willing to change your mind, then God will change your life.

CHAPTER FIVE

From *Asking God to Change the World* to *Praying That He Change Us*

*J*esus said, "Be of good cheer," which is certainly positive. But then he added, "for I have overcome the world." He didn't say, "I have fixed the world," but rather, "I have overcome" it. The difference between fixing the world and overcoming it is huge. The problem most of us have is that we try to fix instead of overcoming, which is why we never find that fundamental good cheer.

Trying to fix the world is like trying to change a movie by manipulating the movie screen. The world as we know it is simply a screen onto which we project our thoughts. Until we change those thoughts, the movie stays the same.

If we want our lives to change, it does little good to simply move from town to town, job to job, or relationship to relationship. Wherever we go, as they say, we take ourselves with us. We manifest not so much according to geography as according to consciousness. We can travel wide, but that of itself will not fundamentally change us. For our lives to change, we must travel deep.

The truth is that our fundamental happiness stems not from anything that happens in the material world, but from love. Certainly there are some wonderful experiences to be had on the material plane, and there is nothing wrong with enjoying them to the fullest. The world itself is neutral; whether or not something of the material plane can be considered holy is determined by the purposes our mind ascribes to it.* That which is used by the Holy Spirit for purposes of genuine healing is holy; that which is used by the ego for purposes of separation is not. The body itself can be a "beautiful lesson in communion until communion is."* Wherever there is love, there is God.

But we cannot enjoy the material plane if we are overly attached to it; the secret of happiness lies in knowing that we are in the world but not of it. That understanding—keeping our thoughts on love while having our feet planted squarely on earth—is the intersection between heaven and earth. And that intersecting point is what we are. It is our mission to live on the earth while thinking only the thoughts of heaven, and when we do, the power of the intersecting point between man and God (symbolized visually in both the cross and the Star of David) overcomes all negative force. That is the overcoming to which Jesus referred and that he himself embodied.

In the Bible it is said that the Holy Spirit will give us a new mind. And who among us could not use that? It becomes fruitless to ask God to change our world once we recognize the world is merely the reflection of our thoughts. What we pray for is the healing of our minds.

It's impossible to make your life new when your mind is running old tapes. Time and time again, we've blown it at exactly the same place in a relationship or sabotaged a professional endeavor in exactly the same way. Yet we feel powerless to stop our self-defeating behavior. What's the point of attracting an opportunity if we're only going to ruin it anyway?

We pay a high price for refusing to accept the part we play in causing our problems; if I don't see I caused it, then I can't see I can change it!* But once I'm willing to take total responsibility for my own experience, I can see the value of inviting the Holy Spirit to enter my mind and fill me with His spirit. Consciousness precedes form, and the perfect form arises from a consciousness of total love.

Total love seems like a very tall order until we consider the reality that total love is what we *are*. So where's the disconnect? We ask, "If I am love, and love creates miracles, then why is my life so screwed up?"

At a certain level it's not our divine reality that's the issue—the issue is how much of that reality we allow ourselves to *experience* and *express*. In the introduction to *A Course in Miracles*, it's stated, "The course does not aim at teaching the meaning of love, for that is beyond what can be taught. It does aim, however, at removing the blocks to your awareness of love's presence, which is your natural inheritance." Love is all around us, but we're in the mental and emotional habit of deflecting it.

With every attitude of attack or defense, we send love away. With every perception of anyone's guilt, we tell love to leave. With every thought of limited possibility, we tell miracles we don't want them. And then we wonder why we're depressed.

To treat the depression, we must ask ourselves essential questions: What am I doing, or not doing, to allow fear rather than love to prevail here? Who am I attacking or not forgiving? What am I myself not giving to this situation? We indulge our fear as if we're being strong to do so, "honest" in a way that makes us more "real." But what is so real about playing weak instead of strong? Sometimes we need to tell our fear to go to hell, which is literally where it came from.

The ego is backed by the weight of an entire thought system, constantly luring us away from love and limitlessness toward fear and scarcity. It is a vicious taskmaster, and it has our hearts—indeed our entire planet—in its grip. And some people would rather die than change their minds.*

The transformation of the heart will take more than an intellectual decision. The ego is a mental addiction to the thinking of fear, and only a spiritual experience can break an addiction. If we want our lives and our world to genuinely change, then we need a spiritual experience to make it happen. And to have that experience, we must open our hearts to receive it.

Trusting the Process

If you don't know there's a force out there working for you, then why would you think to trust it? With all the millions of churches, mosques, temples, and shrines that exist in the world, how many people really think that the God who created the moon and the stars is truly looking out for *them?* Yet there is no unit of time or space, nor element of life, about which the Author of All Things is not actively concerned. He loves you because He loves everything and everyone. He who is Love cannot not love.

What an amazing thought, that ever-unfolding good is actually the natural order of the universe. And we were created to enjoy it. To the ego, that is a preposterous notion; it would have us believe that joy is something lovely to be *outgrown*. But look at small children gleefully at play; do we know something they don't know, or do they perhaps know something we've forgotten? As I listen to my teenage daughter discuss love and relationships, I remember how it was for me when I was her age. I don't look back on my earliest forays into romance and think, "Oh, but that was only puppy love." Rather, I look back and think how courageously we loved, before we knew what there was to be afraid of; how strong we were, before any other agendas stood in the way of our love; and how pure our hearts were, when they were not yet tainted by cynicism or doubt. The older we are, the more we know some things; the younger we are, the more we know others. Age only makes us smarter if we retain our bravery.

Enlightenment is not a learning but an unlearning, a letting go of all the fears we've gathered as we've walked the path of life. As taught in *A Course in Miracles*, "miracles are everyone's right, but purification is necessary first."* Purification is the process by which everything but love dissolves from our mind. As we drop the layers of fear and illusion that have hardened around our psyches, we are left with the love with which we were endowed at our creation.

Just as embryonic cells are programmed to develop into a baby, each of us is programmed to develop a more magnificent life. An invisible hand guides the embryo and guides you and me as well. But unlike the embryo, you and I can refuse it. God didn't create us as babies and then just dump us here and say, "Okay, kid, now you're on your own." But how do we know that, if we're not taught to listen to our hearts? How can we "go with the flow" if we don't know such a flow exists? And so we keep going around saying "No" to life and then wondering why life seems to be saying "No" to us.

The Divine Physician

God knows our crooked places that need to be made straight, the wounds in our hearts that fester for years unhealed, the broken pieces of our lives that seem beyond repair. And He who is the Author of miracles has infinite desire as well as power to heal them all.

So if that's the case, then why so much pain? Could it be that the doctor has the medicine but the patient refuses to take it? According to *A Course in Miracles*, God cannot take away from us what we do not release to him. It's not enough to *understand* your problem, to say, "My mother made me feel unsafe when I was a child, so that's why I react the way I do." Rather, we need to say, "Dear God, I know I react this way. Please change me." And that's an important difference.

At a certain point, it doesn't really matter so much how we got to be a certain way. Until we *admit* our character defects—and take responsibility for the fact that regardless of where we got them, *they are ours now*—God Himself has no power to heal them. We can talk to a therapist for hours about how our relationship with Mom or Dad made us develop a certain behavioral characteristic, but that of itself will not make it go away. Naming it, surrendering it to God, and asking Him to remove it—*that's* the miracle of personal transformation. It won't go away in a moment, necessarily, but its days are numbered. The medicine is in your psychic bloodstream.

Sometimes, therefore, the healing process involves our having to take a good look in the mirror before we can do anything else. You might pray for a better job situation, and the next thing you know, you experience your biggest professional disaster yet. It might seem that when you prayed things only got worse. But what actually happened is that you were moved subconsciously to create a situation in which your own weakness was on display, magnified enough for you to get a very good look at it. Things in fact did not get worse; you were simply no longer anesthetized to your own experience and the part you played in creating it.*

Let's say you finally got the dream job you had been praying for, yet within a couple of weeks of starting it, you began to display the same self-sabotaging behavior that had held you back before. At first you think, "Oh no, this isn't a miracle! It's terrible!" But then you realize, "Oh, wow, I get it. The miracle is that I have a chance, right here and now, to choose again, to stand in the same spot where I have blown it before, and do things another way. I can pray for help in becoming the person who handles this situation with ease and grace." God doesn't help us *avoid* our issues; He *transforms* our issues.

In that sense, when we're in the midst of a spiritual transformation things often seem to get worse before they get better. We usually have to look at what we hate about ourselves before we can see how much there is to love. There is a "ring of fear" around the light within us, through which the ego seeks to block our entrance into the heaven within.*

And that's why we pushed so many issues to the back of the drawer to begin with: so we wouldn't have to endure the pain of genuine self-examination. We're afraid of an ugliness we feel is lurking inside us, but in fact what we fear is an illusionary self. This illusion exudes a continuous toxicity if it remains in the dark, yet disappears the moment it's exposed to light. The ego is dispersed into nothingness when released into the hands of God.

The ego is not where we're bad but where we're wounded. Yet often we don't want to take a good look at our wounds—much less let God look with us—because we're ashamed. No one expects a wound on the body to be pretty—we're not ashamed of the blood and gore accompanying a physical wound—yet we're embarrassed that we have emotional wounds. Our emotional and psychological wounds often appear not as places where we are hurt but rather as places where we are guilty. Our spiritual wounds take the form of character defects.

While it might have been a wounded childhood that caused a negative pattern to begin with, that fact isn't necessarily obvious to others. Only to the miracle-minded does your behavior read, "I was hurt as a child. Have compassion." We're all involved in the same matrix of ego delusion—focusing not on each other's wounds, because they don't appear on the surface, but on each other's faults, because they do.

So we often try to hide who we are rather than heal who we are. We're afraid that if we show our true selves, something ugly will appear. Only when we realize Who lives within us do we see that only beauty will appear. In the meantime, our wounds fester, untended, until surrendered for divine healing. Our denial, or unwillingness to look deeply at our own issues, reflects a naive hope that if we don't look at our wounds, they'll go away by themselves. It takes emotional courage to look deeply into ourselves and face what's there. Until we do, however, God's medicine can't heal us.

Until you understand that God is your healer and not your judge, it's unlikely you will go to Him with your pain. It's understood we take our clothes off if the doctor needs to check us, but we're afraid to present ourselves naked before God. Until we make the switch from the notion of an angry, judgmental God to an all-merciful and forgiving one, we are bound to have an ambivalent relationship to Him. Why would we want to admit our mistakes to someone we think will judge us for them?

We've created a God in our own image: angry and judgmental *because we are.* God Himself is merciful and all-loving, but we have projected onto Him our fear. This separates us from His love, from His healing, and from each other. When we change our perception from a God of wrath to a God of mercy, we will realize God is a divine physician. Our pain is the pain of hell, or separation from love. It isn't God who sends us to hell for being bad, it's God who *delivers* us from hell after the ego *told* us we are bad. Hell is when you think you're a terrible person and you never do anything right; God is the One who reminds you of the innocence in which you were created and to which He will help you return. Hell is when you feel you're a complete and utter failure who will never succeed; God is the One who reminds you that He lives within you and that in Him all things are possible. Hell is when you think you can never escape your past mistakes; God is the One who makes all things new. It is the ego—not God— who casts us into the "fires of hell." It is God who lifts us out of them.

Taking Our Medicine

God knows us as He created us—perfect and innocent now and forever.* Our mistakes don't change our eternal essence, and it's that which the Father knows and loves. Our prayer for healing, for atonement, for correction, is a prayer to be healed of our own forgetfulness. We pray to be *reminded* of who we really are so our thoughts and behavior no longer reflect a dissociation from our divine self.

We can pray before every day, every meeting, every encounter that we will be our best—that we won't be thrown off our center by fear and ego. And afterward, we can surrender every aspect of what occurred—what we felt, what we did, what we're ashamed of, what we're angry about or feeling hopeful about.

We can't fix ourselves, and we don't have to. When we are willing to open ourselves completely to God, showing Him our darkness as well as our light, His spirit enters us at deeper levels than any worldly force could penetrate. Then, and only then, are we changed on causal levels of consciousness, genuinely freed of the patterns that have held us back.

We don't like it when a doctor rushes in for an appointment, spends five minutes with us, and then rushes out. How could he or she possibly understand our situation, the subtle nuances of our predicament? Yet we rush in and rush out of an appointment with the divine physician all the time. We dip in for a prayer here, a bit of meditation there. We read a book of inspirational poems or sayings. We do seminars or go to weekend retreats. But only a continuous change in the way we think is enough to guarantee a spiritual healing. It is not enough to get naked with God every once in a while. We must present ourselves authentically to Him not just sometimes but all the time: not just every hour, but every moment of every day. We can open our hearts so much that all our fear will melt away. We can live in a continuous communion with God in which every perception, every possible thing, is constantly surrendered for His blessing and review. And when we are so radically available to Him, we will find Him radically available to us.

Mercy

Sometimes we walk closely with God, and sometimes we sprint to the other side of the universe. Who among us hasn't taken a few detours into fear?*

Yet when we do, and then come back to love, we learn among other things how merciful God is. There are certain words you can't truly understand until you actually experience them. And *mercy* is one of them.

When I was young, the concept of God's mercy meant little to me; I figured it meant He was "nice." But now I have an appreciation for the concept I could never have had before; you usually have to have lived a while before you understand the meaning of real regret. But I have found that He just keeps using our mistakes, as well as our successes, to turn us into the people He has in mind for us to be.

God's mercy is an active power. His angels, both visible and invisible, are present at every step of our journey, reaching out to us as we reach out to them. Whenever we are receptive to His healing, His healing is on the way; God will do His part if we do ours. As we admit the exact nature of our wrongs, making amends wherever possible; as we atone and ask God to remove our character defects; as we open our hearts to receive His daily comfort and allow Him to use us in bringing comfort to others; as we seek through prayer and meditation to both know His will for us and *do* His will for us, a miraculous process takes place within us. We are lifted from weak to strong; we are lifted from lack to abundance; we are lifted from pain to peace; we are lifted from fear to love. None of this happens in an instant, but over time, through the daily processes of living. In every darkened corner—emotionally, psychologically, spiritually, physically—He sends His light to replace all darkness.

And thus we are redeemed. There is no situation that ties His hands. And there is no person in whom He is not interested or for whom He does not have a plan for their healing. The world as we know it can be cruel indeed, but the redemptive, all-loving power of God is present in the very nature of things.

Redemption

I once spoke at a seminar held for women on probation or parole in the federal justice system. Many had served time—some a long time—in prison. All of them were desperate to lead a new and different kind of life, and they came to the seminar in hopes of learning how. Before I spoke, a woman currently on parole and doing very well told her story. I was mesmerized by her talk, which was a profound and compelling tale of redemption.

Michelle had served five years in jail for a drug-related crime, and at the time of her sentence, her four-year-old son was taken to live with her elderly parents. When she was released from jail, she had her child and very little else. Through an anonymous fellowship and the guidance of her parole officer, she learned slowly and meticulously how to put one foot in front of the other and build a new life. Her struggles—the fact that the only kinds of jobs she could find initially were the lowest paying ones at which she was treated poorly, the initial rejection by prospective employers when they saw on her application that she was a convicted felon, her having to learn to control her anger, her difficulties with an angry young son—were all met with a deep understanding that through the grace of God, and one day at a time, she *could* stay sober, she *could* build a life for herself, and she *could* avoid ever returning to prison. In time she entered college, learned how to succeed as a student, graduated, and then earned her master's degree in social work. As she shared her hope and strength with other women who were wounded in their souls in much the same way that she had been, the light of God, which so clearly had blessed her, extended through her to touch them as well.

Michelle suffered greatly for her mistakes, but she experienced God's mercy and she can bear witness to it now in the lives of others. Sometimes He uses our suffering to hone us, as it makes us more humble, more contrite, and more open to guidance we'd rejected before. Sometimes we come out on the other side of a dark time with an inner knowledge, some sense of the soul we didn't have before. Sometimes the fire we went through becomes our purifying agent, allowing the miracle God had planned for us to seize our hearts and make us new.

And so, could it be that some of the things that hurt us the most were in fact the workings of God's love—like an operation the doctor performs in order to save you? Sometimes difficult experiences have the effect of a storm. Afterwards we see a beauty in the sky and a cleanness in the air that were not there before. What was chaotic at the time had an ultimately salutary effect. And sometimes, when we're really fortunate, we look up in the sky and see a rainbow. It could not have happened without the rain.

Becoming Teachable

Our job is not to *determine* life's meaning but to *discern* its meaning. Often we try to tell life what it means when we would be better off allowing life to *show* us what it means.* When Jesus said we should be as little children, it was because little children know that they don't know.* We go around thinking or at least pretending we know the meaning of things, when in fact the mortal mind has no basis for real knowing. Little children expect someone older and wiser to explain things to them; we can have the same relationship with God.

There's a way of relaxing into our center, working much less hard, letting other people have their say, knowing our being is even more radiant at times when we're in a space of not-doing. When the ego steps back, the power of God can step forward. He can and will, when we allow Him to. Too often we feel we're invisible unless we're making the cool comment, doing this or doing that. But we're so much more powerful when surrounded by silence. Taking a deep breath, knowing that what you don't say can be as powerful as what you do say, thinking deeply about something before making a response—such actions leave room for the spirit to flow, to harmonize your circumstances and move them in a more positive direction. How many times have we felt we've blown it simply by talking when we wish we hadn't or by showing off when we could have just sat there and seemed intriguing—because we *were?*

God's spirit will always reveal the truth to us if we simply don't block His guidance. And we block it by talking first, attitudinally walking ahead of truth. This happens when we push too hard—in a conversation or a project—trying frantically to make things happen, or keep things from happening, because we lack faith in an invisible order of things. That is why the Holy Instant matters: it is a moment of quiet when the spirit enters and makes right all things.

Often it's better to live in a question until the answer emerges; to be okay with not knowing until wisdom comes; to take a backseat and just listen until you genuinely have something to say. Sometimes it is our silence that testifies to our strength.

Our entire being—intellectual, emotional, psychological, and spiritual—can relax into a more miracle-receptive mode. When we relax into the arms of God, the mind opens to greater insight and the heart to deeper love.

When we step back with the ego and let God lead the way, we become a natural space for healing. Let's say, for instance, that you have a problem; many possibilities exist for how you could solve it. Yet if you're tense about the issue, stuck in anger or frantic searching, then the chances of one of those possibilities becoming clear are decreased.

If you have a problem but you are stuck in blaming others or trying to duck out of your own responsibility, then helpful forces are repelled. If you have a problem but you try to keep your heart open—you do your best to deal with it, take personal responsibility, remain vulnerable—then others will have a natural tendency to reach out to you and offer help. Just knowing you have a problem will not inspire others to help you; how you're handling it is what will do that.

Highest solutions don't come from you; they come *into* you and *through* you. It is not your ability to figure things out, put the blame elsewhere, or hire the right lawyers that ultimately guarantees divine right action. Rather, it is our surrender to the flow of divinity that allows divinity to flow through us.

Staying calm and trusting in the flow of the universe are hard when we can't sense a cosmic order to things. Yet once we recognize that God is everywhere, all the time, we can relax into any instant and know that healing is natural. God will exalt us if we will allow Him to. And when we feel that happening, we're liable to smile a certain kind of smile, inspiring someone around us to say, "What?" as though surely there must be something that is making us smile that way. But there is nothing that is making us smile at that moment, so much as *everything* is making us smile. We have sensed Reality and felt the peace that follows.

Strength in Our Defenselessness

The workbook of *A Course in Miracles* includes an exercise that reads, "In my defenselessness my safety lies."

It is astonishing to consider all the defenses we walk around with, emotionally and psychologically. Imagine every moment, from the time you were born, when something seemingly unsafe occurred—a spanking, or a moment of misunderstanding or invalidation. In each instance, you built a defense mechanism— an automatic closing off of the heart—and by the time you were old enough to act out these defenses, you had no conscious awareness that they even existed. Once we've reached out for love enough times and felt unloved in return, we shut down and try to defend ourselves against the blow we subconsciously have come to expect. Often our form of defense is to attack before someone else has a chance to or to intimidate in order to keep our imagined attacker at bay or to try to impress so as not to be rejected.

The problem with this is that we "create what we defend against."* If I have my dukes up, an opponent will surely appear. If I put on grandiose airs in order to impress, I will surely be rejected.

It always feels like we're protecting ourselves when we're wrapped in the ego's energies. Yet in fact, the ego is our weakness and not our strength. When we act defensive or arrogant or willful, no one will think us strong; quite the opposite. It can feel like we're exposed and vulnerable when we stand defenseless and empty before God, yet when we do is when we appear centered and in our power. Our ability to be transparent, to become an empty space through which God's love can flow, is our spiritual strength. When the ego disappears, we are hardly invisible; we're illumined. People can't take their eyes off a person who has removed his or her mask. Childlike serenity replaces childish posturing. We are gentle yet strong. The light within shines through.

As we shift our center of power from material strength to spiritual strength, we begin to change from a "go-out-and-get-'em" kind of personality to a more magnetic "be-centered-and-watch-the-world-come-to-you" kind of personality. The toughness, the intensity, and the assertiveness of the personality are second-rate powers compared to the spirit within. In any moment that we simply breathe deeply, giving up attachment to goal or outcome, living only to enjoy the instant and the love it brings, we are surrendered to God. And in losing ourselves, we find ourselves. At last.

From *A Course in Miracles:*

We will remind ourselves that He remains beside us through the day, and never leaves our weakness unsupported by His strength. We call upon His strength each time we feel the threat of our defenses undermine our certainty of purpose. We will pause a moment, as He tells us, "I am here."*

When New Life Stirs

In all the great religious teachings, there are coded messages from God. Students of enlightenment seek to understand those messages and apply them to our lives. Whether or not a particular religion is our personal path, its core mystical teachings apply to everyone.

In museums across the world there are thousands of paintings of an event described in the New Testament as the Annunciation. The angel Gabriel appeared to the maiden Mary, telling her that she would conceive a child by God, and the child would be born to be savior to the world.

Putting aside for a moment what *that* must have felt like, let's remember that all religious stories represent a deeper metaphysical truth. Angels are the thoughts of God, and Mary isn't the only one who has had angels come and talk to her. Angels are talking to all of us constantly, but most of us don't listen.

Gabriel represents a particular kind of message from God, namely that He wants to impregnate us spiritually, miraculously turn us into new people, and extend His love onto the earth through us. The difference between us and Mary is that she had the humility and grace to say, "Yes."

You and I say, "Thanks, maybe sometime," "Not now," "Be real," "Gimme a break," "No way," and a host of other things that don't exactly resonate with Mary's willingness to be used by God. But those paintings exist, as does all art, to take our minds to the place where we remember what's true. That story is not just about her; it's about us as well.

Around all of us, at every moment, there's an angel heralding a new beginning, the birth of a new being from the pieces of our scattered selves. Every situation represents a choice: do we prefer to stay with ego-based patterns of thought and behavior, or do we choose to play life in a higher, more loving way? Will we tread the path of limitation and fear, though that path has grown painful and boring and old, or do we choose to give birth to a higher mode of expression? The Christ within is a newborn self, fathered by God and mothered by our humanity, here to express the divine potential that exists inside us all.

Mary could not have said "No" to God because it would have been contrary to her nature. And at our deepest core, it's contrary to ours as well. We long to say "Yes" to Him, but we're so out of touch with who we really are, so not in conscious contact with our own souls, that we continually say "No." And there, in that rejection of love, lies the tragedy of human existence.

One day we say, "Yes, God, you can express your love through me." And on another day, in another situation, we just can't make the stretch—we say no to more forgiveness or more depth or more love. Yet Gabriel persists, and every time we say no, he simply waits around to ask us again. "I'm bringing this situation around again to give you another chance."

Slowly but surely, our hearts begin to open; we resist love less, the longer we trod the spiritual path. And ultimately we will resist no longer. If we're deeply, truly honest with ourselves, we know we're longing to be pregnant with God.

When Gabriel spoke to Mary, she was a fourteen-year-old girl, and now he speaks to each of us, no matter what our sex or how old we are. As long as we are willing to be part of God's plan, then God has a plan for us.

And that's when life begins to truly change: not when we have new things, but when we have a new spirit. The birth of God's love into the world is not just a "was," but an "is." It's important not just because of what it did to the world, but because of what it does to us. As we love each other, God lives in us. He overshadows our mind and heart. He guides our thinking, our behavior, and our words. He removes from us our thoughts of fear, miraculously replacing them with thoughts of love. In that lies our holiness, and there is literally nothing our holiness cannot do.*

When the three kings bowed down before the baby Jesus, they symbolically expressed the relative weakness of the powers of the world compared to the power of our true being when we are centered in the love of God. The radiance of the divine child is you and me transformed.

Our fears dissolve, and our energetic armor melts. As we pray constantly for an ever more open heart, the action of God's Spirit redeems our past and frees our future to be unlike it. We are spiritually reborn, as the illusions of the past fall away and we have the chance to begin again.

Sometimes someone will say to us, "You seem like a completely new person."

Sometimes we do seem like a new person. And sometimes, we actually *are* one.

The Christ

The conversion to Christ need not entail a conversion to the Christian religion. The word is a symbol for the Child of God within us, our true identity and a space of remembrance of all that is divine. To be His disciple is to take on the mantle of His ministry by refusing to acknowledge the ultimate reality of any walls that divide us. In our oneness with others lies our oneness with God, and removing those walls is His work in us and in the world. God's one begotten son is *who we are*.

So it is that we seek to see with the eyes of God's son, in which only our unity with others is seen; to hear with the ears of God's son, where only love and calls for love are heard; to walk with Him, to wherever we can be of service; and to speak for Him of our love for everyone.

Try thinking of a situation in your life where things aren't going as you wish. Now close your eyes and take a deep breath, and allow yourself to see yourself as you dwell within that experience. See how you look, your mannerisms, and your normal behavior. See how others relate to you. Feel all your feelings as they arise, even if they are painful or anxious.

Now see Jesus, as the embodiment of Christ, come up behind you and put His arms around you. He has been given by God the power to make you whole. Allow him to permeate your being and to heal every broken part of you. Allow Him to stand in the breach for you, between the you now manifest and your divine potential. He *is* that potential, and He has been given by God the power to help anyone who asks for His help to actualize it within themselves.

He is as clear in the Holy Instant as we allow him to be.* Either He's *metaphorically* there, or He's *literally* there. Which it will be in your experience is completely up to you.

The changes that spirit accomplishes within us cannot be explained to the ego mind, but looking to the ego for either approval or verification is ridiculous. We think that without the ego all would be chaos, but in truth, without the ego all would be love.* At some point, you must decide which way of looking at the world makes the most sense; you can't just kinda-sorta embrace a mystical reality. The spiritual life involves believing in an invisible reality that affects a visible one. As we change within, we change our behavior. We change our energy. We change our lives.

Creating Miracles

Centered in an attitude of blessing, we become automatic miracle workers. People feel uplifted and energized along with us, subconsciously corrected and healed in our presence. A palpably more positive atmosphere prevails. When we reach for the highest within ourselves, people around us feel called to their highest. And that is the beacon for which every soul is looking.

As we remember our spiritual heritage and stand within its power, we think, act, and then experience all of life differently. We're about to judge someone, and then we remember their eternal innocence. We're about to share an unkind story we heard about someone, and then we remember, "What I do to others I am doing to myself." We're about to reach for a win at another person's expense, and we remember that there is no such thing. We are complaining about a situation, and we stop to ask ourselves, "What am *I* not contributing here?" *This* is the birth of our better selves—a gradual and continuous process, as in any given moment we either listen to the ego or we listen to love.

Whichever we listen to is what we will become. And whatever we become is the world we will inhabit. We can live in fear, or we can live in love. And every moment, we decide. The greatest power God has given us to change the world is the power to change our thoughts about the world.* And as we do, the world transforms.

No matter how insane the world might appear, we seek to remember it's a vast illusion. We don't become more metaphysically complicated as we do this; in fact, we become simpler and simpler, trying to apply certain basic principles to everything we go through. We know there is a world of love that lies beyond what we see, and we were born to make it manifest. If we apply ourselves body and soul to the task, then one day—right here on earth—we will experience an illumined world.

CHAPTER SIX

From *Living in the Past and Future* to *Living in the Present*

*I*f we want to change worlds, then we have to change time slots.

There's no point in trying to watch *Seinfeld* at 8:00 if it's on at 7:00. And there's no point in trying to find miracles in the past or future when they only exist in the present.

I always used to wonder what my future would be like. When I was done obsessing about the future, I would be content for about five minutes, and then I would begin to obsess about the past. It's clear the ego has no intention of letting us enjoy the present.

And that's because the present is holy ground—the only place where eternity meets linear time. The past is nowhere except in your mind, and the future is nowhere except in your mind. The ego is intent on having us live in one of those two realms as a way of making sure we never *live at all*. If God dwells only in the present, then living in the past or future is bound to be painful because it leaves Him out. Living fully in the present, the Holy Instant, is literally death to the ego—and that is why we resist it. As long as we identify with the life of the ego, reality itself seems scary.

We find it easier to analyze what happened in the past and to imagine what might happen in the future than to show up fully for life in the present. Yet when we allow ourselves to fully *be*, unencumbered by past or future concerns, that moment becomes our portal to the miraculous, Harry Potter's platform no. $9^{3}/_{4}$. The Holy Instant *is* the miracle.

When the Bible says, "Time shall be no more," it doesn't mean the end of the world, it means the end of the illusion of linear time and the beginning of an eternal now.

The things that are most important are everlasting. *Everlasting* doesn't refer to some eternal reality that begins when this life is over and some other life begins. It refers to a moment-by-moment reality that has gone on forever, is true this instant, and will endure forever. *Everlasting* means "always true."

Eternity means a never-ending present in which God *is*. It is the dimension of His power, and to the extent that we use the present to focus on past or future, we disempower ourselves. The tennis player doesn't have time to think about the ball he or she just missed because it would take away from the effort to hit the next one. It is the same with all of us, all the time.

The past doesn't automatically blend into the future except in our minds. The past leads to the future simply because we allow it to; it is more a product of the way our brains function than of the way reality functions. By thinking about the past in the present, we simply recreate it in the future.

Yet a miracle can intercede between past and future, releasing each moment to endless new possibilities. In the Holy Instant, we can break the chain of yesterday's thought, reprogramming the future by thinking different thoughts today. A common mistake is to base our thoughts on yesterday's circumstances, not realizing that those circumstances are simply the reflection of thoughts we're now free to change.

Let's say you're thinking, "I'm broke." That might be a description of a material condition, yet material conditions change in response to a change in consciousness. To affirm "I'm broke" is to choose to extend the condition into the future by thinking it in the present. And if that is your choice, then the universe will respond, "So be it." But you might want to ask yourself why you choose to think that, considering how much power you have to change your circumstances by changing your thoughts. I heard the spiritual teacher Chalanda Sai Ma once say, "You will experience whatever you think after the words 'I am . . .'"

You could instead think, "I am infinitely abundant in spirit. I have lots of money (money is a relative concept: most Americans who think they're broke have more money than the majority of the world's population), and my fortune is growing every day." Notice how just *saying* that instructs your body as well as your mind. Saying "I'm broke" will send one kind of signal through the brain; saying "I'm wealthy" will send another. Brain chemicals, hormones, and an endless array of mental and physical functions respond to every thought. It's hard to say "I'm broke" with your spine straight and your head up; it's hard to say "I'm wealthy" in any other way. The subconscious mind is your servant, responding to your every command. And how you feel and how you present yourself will affect your material circumstances in countless ways.

Perhaps a lover or two rejected you, so now you think, "I have no luck in love; my partners leave me." But in fact, what you're probably saying is that *some* people left you while others would have overcharged their credit cards to have tea with you in Timbuktu.

But your ego just *loves* to go for that negative thought! That's the same ego that set you up to fail with the ones who left, now contextualizing the situation in such a way as to make sure it happens again. The ego's dictate in love is "Seek, but do not find."*

You could say to yourself instead, "I'm totally attractive, and the most wonderful people in the world think I'm the most wonderful person to be with." And you know why? Because the most wonderful people for you really would think that! But your thoughts that such people don't exist, or would reject you, are literally keeping them at bay. There is no magnetic force calling them toward you if you deny that they exist.

If you're thinking thoughts like, "Men reject me," then I doubt your energy is exactly reading, "Hot babe." If your energy just confirms a past condition, then expect the condition to remain. But you can inwardly prepare for what you want rather than always affirming what has been. You can *practice* the life you want. "If life *were* what I wanted it to be today, what would I think and do? Where would I go? How would I handle myself?" It's like the movie *Field of Dreams:* "If you build it, they will come." Time and space are not what they appear to be; you are not at their effect unless you choose to be. God placed you on the earth to be a master of your own destiny, not a slave to the material world.

It helps to ask ourselves why we choose to play so small when we don't have to. Belief is powerful, and whatever we believe, we will subconsciously make manifest. So why do we hold on to core beliefs about ourselves that are so demeaning? When we ask that question, the answers emerge: "My family told me it wasn't okay to think I was a big deal." "I thought people wouldn't like me if I 'had it all.'" "I thought it might hurt my father's feelings if I made more money than he did."

Yet whatever pain we might experience at others' negative reactions to our spreading our wings, is nothing compared to the pain we cause ourselves by clipping them. At this time on the planet, no one can feel good about withholding their magnificence. Expressing your full potential is not just your right; it's your responsibility.

As long as you keep thinking in limited terms, disbelieving in the possibility of infinite possibility in your life, then you will never experience the miracles God has in store for you. You will deny His gifts, taking on the ego's servitude instead. In a world such as this, fear is often the path of least resistance. If you want a miracle, you have to consciously *claim* it. And for everyone out there who might say, "How dare you?" there are at least two more who will say, "Thank you for showing me how."

Embracing the Real

Sometimes I hear people say, "I'm ready to change my thinking, but I'm afraid that others around me won't change theirs, so it won't do any good." Perhaps, but not for long. As soon as you change your mind, others will begin to change theirs, and those who do not will begin to fall away.

I was having a conversation with a young man, Andrew, who was about to reenter his hometown high school after having attended an out-of-town school for two years. He was depressed about returning home, and I asked him why.

"I was such a jerk when I lived here before. I was really insecure, and so I acted like a big know-it-all. I'm sure everyone here just thinks of me as this total loser, and going back to that is really depressing."

"But have you changed?" I asked him. "Are you different now?"

"Yeah," he said. "But *they* don't know that. They just know me as I was back then, so it doesn't matter that I've changed. No one there will like me."

"Well, actually," I told him, "from a metaphysical perspective, all minds are joined. So if *you've* changed, then *they've* got to change. The other kids might think of you a certain way at first, but if you've truly changed, then everything but who you are now will drop away. If you don't take the old stuff with you, then it won't be able to stay in their minds except for a very short time."

The universe is primed to start over again in any moment, and it is only our own thoughts to the contrary that keep it from doing so. A miracle occurs when we ask God to intervene between our past and future, cancel out all fear, and release us to new beginnings. A God who will part the seas and raise the dead has no difficulty solving your problems in high school—or anywhere else, for that matter. His is a radical power to repair and restore. When our faith is as audacious and radical as His power, we will experience that power to the fullest.

Spiritually, we are reborn in any moment we do not take the past with us.* My young friend Andrew and I prayed that day, asking God to take his relationship with his schoolmates into His hands. We asked Him to remove all walls of misunderstanding. We prayed that his relationships would be reborn, that he might start over in a different place. We asked for divine right order, in this and all things.

A few weeks later I saw Andrew again. He smiled at me and gave me a really big hug. "Had a miracle, huh?" I asked him. "Oh, yeah," he said. "*Oh,* ye-ah . . ."

Every moment is part of a divine curriculum, and if I experienced a lack of love in the past, then the present contains ways to compensate for it now. God is ever-present; His hand is on everything. Whatever situation we are in *now*, whatever person or people we are relating to *now*, contains the key to both healing the past and releasing the future. We can be someone different than we were in the past, releasing the future to be different as well.

If we release our past to God, He will change our minds about it for us.* Since only love is real and nothing else exists, the only reality about our past is the love we gave and the love we received.* Everything else is an illusion and will stay alive in our experience only if we choose to hold on to it. According to *A Course in Miracles,* "Nothing real can be threatened; nothing unreal exists." And that is the miracle: to embrace the real.

Healing the Past

When we go through difficult experiences, we have a natural tendency to want to talk about them. And to some extent, that's good; processing with counselors and friends is one of the ways we heal. Yet there is another tendency, of the ego rather than the spirit, that leads us to articulate negative experiences in a way that keeps them alive.

In a town I once visited, I had an experience that was very painful, and when my friends asked me what happened, I would tell them the story. But then I said to myself, "Enough already. It wasn't all bad; think of the wonderful people you met and all the good things that happened there too." So then when friends would ask, I would tell them the negative *and* the positive. But after a while, when I had done my forgiving and atoning and allowed my heart to heal, I found myself answering a query about that period of my life very simply: "It was a special time." The words just came out of my mouth; I didn't consciously realize I was about to say them. But at the deepest level, those words were true because only love exists. Just saying them gave comfort to my heart.

Everything that happens has a cause: either it was caused by love and offers a chance to increase that love, or it was caused by fear, and spirit is present in the situation to lead us out of it. One way or another, as people say these days, "It's all good."

Accepting Ourselves in the Present

When I was younger I wanted to be older, and when I got older I wanted to be younger. When I was living in one place I wanted to live in another, and when I was doing one thing I wanted to be doing something else. I could never just settle into who I was and what was happening at the moment. It seemed that somehow I wasn't enough, what I was doing wasn't enough, and therefore my life was never enough.

I once mentioned in a lecture that I recently looked at a picture of myself when I was thirty and said to myself, "I thought *this* was *inadequate?*" I watched the room fill up with knowing smiles from every woman who was past her youth. Who among us has not looked back on a period we thought was lacking, wishing we could go back to it now and experience the wonders we couldn't see at the time? The truth is that every stage of our lives is perfect, if we allow ourselves to really *live* in it. If we concentrate on the present, contributing and showing up for it as fully as we can, then any moment can have its blessings, and the future will unfold in the direction of ever greater good.

When we accept ourselves exactly as we are, and where we are, we have more energy to give to life. We are not wasting our time trying to make things different. Any moment that we relax into the deeper ground of our being, giving up all struggle to be any-where else, we're in exactly the right place at exactly the right time. There is a plan for our lives—God's plan—and it oversees exactly where we are and where we need to be going. As soon as we have learned to live most brightly in our present conditions, new and better ones will arrive immediately. But until we learn the lessons of the present, they will simply reappear in new guises, and it will seem as though nothing ever changes.

It's not up to us what we learn, only whether we learn through joy or through pain.* But if we don't yet trust that every situation is a lesson, we don't bother to ask ourselves what the lesson *is*. And unless we do, our chances of learning it are nil. Then the lesson will reappear—with ever higher stakes—until we learn it. We may as well learn it the first time, when the chance to learn through joy is still available. The more times a lesson has to come around, the more pain it will generate. If you know in your heart that something is wrong, then ignoring it won't make it any less so. It will simply make fixing it even harder, when it is brought about by a louder noise than the origi-nal sound of God's whisper in your ear.

Handling Joy

Sometimes we do receive joy but then don't quite know how to handle it. At times in my life I had what it took to *attract* my good, but not what it took to *be* with it once it got here. Wonder-ful change was offered me, but I was too nervous to let it in. The suddenness of an opportunity, or the speed by which I was expected to make a decision about it, sort of blew my wattage and I couldn't respond. Sometimes a change presents an opportunity too at odds with our self-perception—too big, too good, too powerful. If God wants to move us in a more positive direction, but we're not yet agreeing with His positive attitude about us, then we will resist His love and resist the blessing. The days when we realize we threw away a miracle can be among the saddest days of our lives.

Once I was walking through a resort community with my fourteen-year-old daughter and her friends. The girls kept a bit ahead of me, needing a little distance and independence from Emma's mom. I didn't feel left out, as the distance felt appropriate for them and for me as well. Motherhood takes up so much of your energy for a few years; as children grow up you begin to get parts of your life back that were put on hold for a while. But as I walked behind the teenagers, I remembered the times my daughter would cling to me so tightly when she was a little girl, needing me every moment, wanting my attention to be centered on her alone. At times I subtly resisted her, feeling smothered by her overwhelming need for attention, as if I were afraid I would be swallowed up by the experience. For a while I could not surrender totally to motherhood, fully accepting that each moment of it was perfect and would transform with time into something else.

I see now that the fact it was happening meant it was exactly what I was supposed to be doing, and I wasn't losing out on anything by giving most of my attention to her. I remember she used to hate my telephone—and for good reason, because I would use it to distract myself from the intimacy of the mother-child connection. I remember once when she was a baby, she actually crawled over to the phone while I was on it, using her little finger to push the button that disconnected the call.

Now the days of her early childhood are over and will not be coming back. During those years I showed up emotionally at about 90 percent of my capacity, perhaps a little more. She may not have missed a lot, but I think I missed a few things. It's all a part of the mistakes you make when you don't recognize that the present moment is perfect.

What Will Be

Obsessing about the future, of course, is just as neurotic as obsessing about the past. It's simply another way the ego robs us of the joy of living by directing our attention away from the present. Living in the future is a way of avoiding life right now.

As miracle workers, we place the future in the hands of God.* We can release our future concerns by living fully in the present, knowing that as we do so, the future will take care of itself. God so clothed the lilies of the field; surely He will take care of us.

I remember how obsessed I used to get, wondering what my life would be like in the future. Now that my past self's future is here, I regret having wasted any time thinking about it at all when such a glorious present was available to me then. I didn't realize at the time that the present was glorious, of course; I was focused on what I perceived to be lacking. And that's the mind game that will continue forever if we allow it to. In the past I didn't realize how perfect things were, just as I don't always realize how perfect they are now. If I had simply allowed myself to *enjoy* my life more, I would have ended up better off later on. And when I allow myself to simply *enjoy* my life right now, I'm giving myself the biggest boost for the future. Every point in life's journey is inherently preparing us for our future in ways the rational mind cannot possibly comprehend.

Yet the thinking of the world is so devoid of any concept of mystery that it's no wonder we can't relax into it. We think we have to lead, when all we really have to do is follow. In whatever moment I'm deeply surrendered to what *is* in life, then what *will be* is programmed to reflect my faith and trust.

Once I was visiting New York with my daughter. We were having a wonderful time, and then she turned to me and said, "I'm so excited about going to Boston next week, I can hardly stand it!" I didn't want to rain on her parade or make her feel invalidated for wanting to go to Boston. But I did muse about how the ego works: always making us think that where we're going next week will be better, what we're doing at the next job will be more right for us, and so forth. Joy can be found only one place at one time: right here, right now. Regardless of where we're going tomorrow, it's important to bless where we are and enjoy the fruits of today. The truth is, almost any experience can be miserable if you're good enough at making yourself miserable. And almost any experience can be enjoyable if you're good enough at practicing joy.

Sometimes people think they can't relax about the future because they need to know what it will be first. I've known people who seemed to think God should send a letter, telling them exactly where to go and what to do. "Dear Gloria, this is God. I've chosen Kansas City for you, where you will live for six months starting this November and work at Carter and Associates. From there you will move to Newport Beach, where you will meet your soul mate. You'll be rich and successful and happy. And then, after a long, long time you will die." They wonder why, if God is so smart, He doesn't use Fed Ex.

But I think we're told so little about the future because there's so much more to understand about the present. God's ground, after all, is *now*. He doesn't spell out the path ahead; rather, He spells out the path within. And as we follow that path, seeking to deepen in our compassion and understanding and capacity to enjoy what is, we co-create with Him our highest future.

Past Regrets

Until you reach a certain age, the word *regret* has little meaning. It's only when you see that your mistakes *did* affect the rest of your life and realize that the bad decisions you made can't be reversed in this lifetime that you face the horror of true remorse. Therein lies the paradox: as human beings, we have such a short period of time here in which to get it right, yet as spirits living in eternity, we have opportunities unlimited. As beings with free will, we are allowed to make our own choices; as children of God, we are redeemed upon our humble and prayerful request, should those choices have been wrong-minded.

Our mistakes are not sins God wants to punish but rather errors He wants to correct. One prayer in *A Course in Miracles* suggests that we simply go back to the moment of our mistake—realizing it was a moment when, by definition, we didn't allow the Holy Spirit to make our decision for us—and allow Him to make it for us now. For miracles work retroactively. There's no need to feel guilty in such a case because the Holy Spirit will undo all the consequences of our wrong decision if we let Him.*
As long as we genuinely atone for our errors, the universe will be miraculously reconfigured on our behalf. Millions of people—alcoholics, drug addicts, people who committed crimes, people

who hurt others—can testify to the profound forgiveness of God. Many know they wouldn't be alive today were their God not such a merciful God.

That means so much for those of us who have lived a lot of years; for those of us who have made huge mistakes that affect ourselves and others for years or even a lifetime; for those of us who can't get over our feelings of guilt about this or that. Like prodigal sons, those of us who have deviated most from love are not relegated by God to the periphery of meaning. Quite the opposite; the Father of the prodigal son didn't reject his son but rejoiced to see him come home. Our mistakes are sometimes what it takes to make us humble, and that's when we're most of use to Him. To God we're never damaged goods. He turns our scars into beauty marks.

Stuck in the Middle

I found turning fifty harder than I expected it to be.

Somewhere around two or three months before the big day, I started to be haunted by memories of a youth now irrevocably over. As much as I told myself that fifty is the new forty, what I really wanted in my heart was to have the old forty back. I had waking nightmares of blazing memories—things I hadn't handled well, stupid choices I had made and could not make over, chances I thought were never more to be retrieved. Grieving the glory of my younger years, I had to face myself and all the pain that comes with it.

Several friends told me they had experienced the same thing, but not to worry—all of a sudden the anxiety would lift. And indeed that is the way it happened for me. Sitting at an outside café late on the night of my big five-O, looking up at the Eiffel Tower lit up against the sky, I felt the pain lift. In an instant, it was all okay. I knew the sun had set on what was no longer, but I had a sense that something new would now dawn to take its place.

Girlfriends had told me that the fifties are great because you don't care anymore what others think. I don't know if that will be true for me, but I do know that I'm not who I used to be. Fifty is as different from forty as forty is from thirty and thirty from twenty. With the coming of fifty, one makes a transition as fundamental as that of puberty. I have settled into the paradox of middle age.

On one hand, I finally have some sense of what I'm doing in the world. At last I'm convinced I have a right to be here. I'm not as frantic as I used to be, though I can't tell yet whether that's because I've evolved or just aged. On the other hand, I get tired more easily, I often can't remember things, and I'm exhausted from just looking for my glasses all the time! Most disconcerting of all, when I'm in a serious mood and I do the math, I can't garner much hope of changing things on this planet during the time I have left. Our generation's shared delusion that we would usher in paradise has been completely shattered. The older you get, the more you see how entrenched certain negatives are. There is so much cruelty in the world that you thought for years would go away; as you age, it dawns on you that it never really does.

As disillusioning as it is to realize these things—and disillusionment is actually a good thing because it means you were laboring under illusions before*—it's also the beginning of spiritual insight. Once you're deeply convinced there are no ultimate answers outside yourself, you start looking for them where they truly are: inside. And you realize that in your slowing down, you're more prepared to listen to things you were moving too fast before to hear.

So much wasted time, so many stupid mistakes. You feel you have the knowledge now, but you're not sure you have the energy left: if only you had known then what you know now. You come to understand George Bernard Shaw's comment, "Youth is wasted on the young."

Our adrenal glands decimated, our cells like fast cars beginning to show wear, the fastest generation has begun to slow down. Jack Nicholson said in a recent interview, "My generation is the new old." Our deepest burden is the accumulated sorrow, the heartbreak of one decade impinging upon the next until the heart can absorb no more. Your mind has figured so much out, but your body isn't sure that it cares anymore. When it's more depressing than joyful to wake up in the morning, then you know you have a problem.

And many do.

Most people, once they hit middle age, face a fork in the road. Which road they take, as Robert Frost wrote, will make all the difference. One road leads to gradual dissolution—a cruise (however slow) toward death; the other road becomes a birth canal, a pattern of rebirth. The older we get, the harder it is to choose rebirth. The ego's gravity seems harder to resist.

We start out so enthusiastic about life, so entertained and delighted by the very nature of things. But the newness fades; we grow jaded or exhausted, and we begin to lose some vital appreciation of the possibilities inherent in a day. As I write this, I hear teenagers in my backyard, delighting in the mud puddles produced by the afternoon's storm. I have to consciously check myself—to remind myself that the ability to have fun in the mud is what makes being young so wonderful, and not make a stink about the fact that my towels are beige and this could ruin them. My mortal truth is that I want the kids to hose off before they come back into the house, but my soul's truth is that I wish I could enjoy the mud too.

So it's completely up to me, whether I start to become an old biddy who cares too much about the towels or instead hold on to my sense of adventure. I want to focus on what's important as I grow older. So what the hell, the kids are happy and that *is* what's important! And not just for kids, but for all of us.

Choosing to See

Birth is audacious; creativity is audacious; the spiritual quest is audacious. Without audacity, we're mere cogs in the wheels of the ego's status quo. And that status quo leads to decay and death, not as a portal to greater life but as a mockery of life itself.

I was once about to throw out what I thought of as dead pink roses when a friend of mine said to me, "What are you doing? Why are you throwing those away?" I said, "They're dying!" He said, "Look at them, Marianne! They're beautiful! I think the faded pink on them today is actually more wonderful than the brighter pink they had yesterday!"

And he was right. It was not the look of the drying flowers but rather my own prejudice that led me to look at the flowers quickly, say, "They're dying," and simply throw them out. In actuality, they were not less beautiful so much as beautiful in a different way. It was not the flowers but my own eyes that needed to change.

In that situation, the flowers had had an *advocate:* my friend, a noted environmentalist, who simply had a more sophisticated eye. The more we live, the more capacity we have to see how much of life is beautiful. There are things that touch my heart now—lovers holding hands, small children laughing—that I barely noticed in days gone by.

I have a friend who worked for a middle-aged rock star, and he told me a story about an experience they once had together. I had been complaining that after a certain point in life it's hard to get excited about a lot of things that used to seem glamorous and fun. My friend said, "Let me tell you about a trip I took with John to Minneapolis.

"We were going there to see a Springsteen concert, and John rented a private jet to fly us from New York. Three of us who work for him piled into a limo and were driving to the airport when one of John's friends called on the phone.

"John exclaimed to him, 'Oh, Ben, you should be here! We're having *so much fun!* We're in a *stretch limo,* and we're going off in a *jet* to a *Springsteen* concert!' John was like an excited little boy, studying the traveler's guide to find a great restaurant in Minneapolis, excited about this trip as though it were the coolest thing in the world."

The point, of course, is that John has been in hundreds if not thousands of private jets; he has been to hundreds if not thousands of rock concerts, including his own; and a stretch limo to him is like a normal car to the rest of us. He travels the world like it's his own backyard, yet here he was studying the travel guide as though Minneapolis were some exotic destination. Apparently, everywhere John goes is exciting to him because he hasn't lost his capacity for joy. Boredom is not his frame of mind.

So then it makes more sense why he's so exciting to the rest of us: he generates fun. He's not waiting for the world to provide it;

he carries it with him. It's an emotional and mental habit he has cultivated.

My father had it. I never saw him bored. And that, I think, is because he wasn't looking for the world to entertain him. Which is precisely why it always did.

I try to remind myself, whenever I am tempted to think the world is boring, "No, Marianne, *you're* boring." And that seems to fix it. Only what we are not giving can be lacking in any situation.* The excitement isn't out there; it's in here, in all of us, when it is what we consciously choose to see.

Rebirth

A friend of mine, a man fifty-seven, said to me once, "I think I'm waiting to die." I understood what he meant, but I responded, "Well, I'm not. I took the other road. I am busy being born."

Thousands of years ago, before the earth was fully populated, there was no reason to live longer than thirty-five or forty years. When we arrived at that age, we had already served the grand purpose of human evolution, the survival of our species. Our sperm and ovaries aged, and as far as nature was concerned, there really was no further need for us to be here. That was the time when physical procreation was the highest purpose of human existence.

Women—perhaps more than men—feel nature's message within our cells: "Thanks. You can go now." Menstrual periods fade away. Doctor's reports come back: "You're done." Pregnancies we so zealously avoided seem clearly now to have been blessings we did not appreciate at the time. We grieve our unborn children, and we grieve our stupid, ungrateful youth.

Nature no longer cares whether we look good, for our attracting sexual partners is of no concern to it anymore. We silently freak. *What happened to my radiance? My voluptuousness? My breasts?* Nature no longer cares to aid our sexual adventures, for whether or not we have sex is of no concern to it anymore. We silently grieve. *What happened to my body? My libido? My juices?* When nature has clearly had its way with us on a certain level, then why are we here? Have we just entered oblivion's waiting room? To whom can we scream? With whom can we cry?

Nature is most concerned with the propagation of the species, and when we're young, our eggs and sperm are our most vital contributions to the process. Yet at this point in human history, the birth of wisdom is more critical for the survival of humanity than the birth of many more children. What we can birth from the womb of our consciousness is every bit as precious a gift to the world as what we can birth from the womb of our bodies. There are a lot of ways to be mother or father to a new world.

Our greatest contribution to the world at this time is not just what we do but who we are becoming. It's the nature of our thinking that is forging a new consciousness. Just as the beginnings of terrorism were rumbling underneath the surface, and thus below the radar, for years before they burst into view, so a new movement of love is rumbling underneath the surface today. Martin Luther King Jr. said we have a "glorious opportunity to inject a new dimension of love into the veins of our civilization." And all of us can participate in this process. Every single moment, with the nature of our thoughts, we can add to love's storehouse in a way that blesses the world.

Yet no spiritual change will ultimately matter if it doesn't reach into our cells and become a very human one as well. I recently heard from a young male colleague that he was enthusiastic about a team of humanitarian activists we had met, "except that it's four white middle-aged women."

I paused. "And the problem with that is . . . ?"

"Well, you know," he said.

And no, I did not know. I understood his political correctness, his wanting racial diversity, but I also saw something else behind this. Many people these days rush to do ceremonies "honoring the wisdom of the grandmothers" but still don't really want to deal with the real-life grandmothers in their midst. They proclaim "the rise of the feminine" but still resist and judge actual women. It's not enough to just honor an *archetype*. If the world is to change, we've got to honor each other. And those who are forging a new future for the world, at whatever age, deserve from themselves, and from those around them, all the honor in the world.

Let's forgive the past and who we were then. Let's embrace the present and who we're capable of becoming. Let's surrender the future and watch miracles unfold.

CHAPTER SEVEN

From *Focus on Guilt*
to *Focus on Innocence*

*I*magine your life as a long-running movie. Now see it made by two different directors. The first movie, in the hands of one director, is a movie about fear, anger, scarcity, and anxiety. The other, in the hands of a different director, is a movie about love, peace, abundance, and happiness.

One director is your ego; the other is the Holy Spirit. And the star of the movie is you.

Because my own life has gone back and forth so much between depressing and uplifting drama, I have a good sense of the difference between the two—and how each is created. One thing I'm clear about regarding both is that when I've looked up close, I've seen these words: "Produced by Marianne Williamson; Directed by Marianne Williamson; Starring Marianne Williamson."

Which director you take your cues from depends on one thing: the thoughts you hold in your mind. To take directions from your ego, all you have to do is focus on guilt. The ego's cornerstone thought is that the child of God is guilty.* To take your direction from the Holy Spirit, focus instead on innocence. Love's cornerstone thought is that the child of God is innocent.*

Whichever focus we choose—on someone's innocence or on their guilt—determines the drama that unfolds in our lives and the part that we play in it.

The Willingness to See

It is our willingness to see the innocence in a person that allows us to see it. The ego mind is so invested in the human drama—"He did this, she said that"—that it often takes a higher power to counterbalance the ego's insistence. It helps to remember that the ego's true target is you: your ego wants you to see guilt in others mainly so you might stay convinced of all the guilt in yourself. The perception of guilt in anyone is our surefire ticket to hell. Every time we blame another, we are tightening the chains that keep our own self-hatred in place.

Forgiveness can be very hard when someone has acted horribly. But the truth, whether or not we care to admit it, is that someone did what we too might have done if we had been as freaked out by something as they were; if we had been as scared of something as they were; if we had been as limited in our understanding as they were. That doesn't mean they shouldn't be held accountable or that we shouldn't have boundaries and standards. It doesn't even mean we have to stay in contact with that person. But it does mean we can come to understand that humanity is not perfect. Just knowing that—that we all do the best we know how with the skills we have at the time—is a realization that opens the heart to more enlightened understanding. And that's what we're on the earth for, because in the presence of people with enlightened understanding, darkness ultimately turns into light.

Forgiveness isn't usually an event; it's a process. An abstract principle has to penetrate various levels of thought and feeling before arriving at the heart, and that's okay. Our hurt can be real, and our feelings matter. The only thing God is asking of us is that we be *willing* to see the innocence in another person. As long as we are willing to see a situation in another light, the Holy Spirit has room to maneuver.

With every human encounter, we either affirm for people their innocence or fortify their guilt. And whichever it is is how we ourselves will feel. We cannot escape our oneness, even if we do not acknowledge it. Do unto others what you would have them do unto you, because they will. And even if they don't, you will feel as though they did.

Because all minds are joined, whatever I choose to think about you I am in essence thinking about myself. To the extent to which I perceive your guilt, I am bound to perceive my own. It doesn't feel that way at first, of course, because the ego would have us believe that as soon as we place the blame on someone else we'll feel better. But that's just a temporary delusion—something the ego specializes in. Once we get over the temporary high of having cast the blame away from us, it will come back to us a hundredfold. An attack thought is like a sword we think we're dropping on someone else's head, when in fact it's dropping on our own.* Only if I'm willing to be easier on others will I ever learn how to be easier on myself.

Think of the things in your life you've gotten away with: things you're ashamed to think about, that you regret, or that you would do over again if you could. And now think how hard you can be on others whose mistakes are similar and sometimes even smaller than your own. Can it be that you want them to pay for what you think you haven't paid enough for? Think about how guilt is binding you to the past. Wouldn't we all want the freedom to begin again that forgiveness alone can bring? Any of us can have that freedom if we are willing to grant forgiveness to others.

Within the world, there are often very serious things we have to forgive. Forgiveness begins, as do all issues of enlightenment, as merely an intellectual concept that has yet to make its "journey without distance" from the head to the heart. It often takes a while to become integrated into our emotional nature. It seems to run counter to reason that we would choose to see the innocence in a person beyond their mistake, yet that is the visionary, as well as most powerful, aspect of faith. Our *experience* of a person might be that they mistreated us, while our *faith* is that they remain an innocent child of God.

No matter what we do to change our lives and to create new possibilities, the bridge to a new life is impossible unless we're willing to forgive. A woman might have been divorced by her husband yet left with enough money to live in a beautiful home, travel the world, and do whatever else she wants for as long as she lives. But until she finds it in her heart to forgive him and bless his path although it swerved away from her, she will live in hell although she lives in a castle. None of that is easy, ever. But unforgiveness is a poison to the soul.

Radical forgiveness is not a lack of discernment or the product of fuzzy thinking. It is a "selective remembering."* We choose to remember the love we experienced, and to let go the rest as the illusion it really was. This doesn't make us more vulnerable to manipulation or exploitation; in fact, it makes us less so. For the mind that forgives is a mind that is closer to its true nature. The fact that I forgive you doesn't mean you "won." It doesn't mean you "got away with something." It simply means I'm free to go back to the light, reclaim my inner peace, and stay there.

Sin versus Error

The world of guilt is based on one notion: the reality of "sin." *Sin* is an archery term that means we missed the mark. We send forth a thought, and sometimes we "miss" the loving bull's-eye. All of us miss the mark of God's love over and over and over again.

Who among us is the right-minded, love-centered, all-forgiving person we would like to be twenty-four hours a day? None of us, but we're on the earth to learn how to be.* God's desire, when we fall short, is not to punish us but to correct us and teach us how to do better. What we think of as our sins were mental miscreations, and though some of our errors are grave, even wicked, there is no end to God's forgiveness and love.

When someone makes an error, we're often tempted to focus all our attention on that person's wrongdoing, even if we previously experienced their goodness. The ego is like a scavenger dog, ever on the lookout for the slightest bit of evidence that someone has made a mistake or wronged us in any way.* *Notice how much less vigilance we apply to seeking out the good in people.* The ego mind is on an instinctive rampage to find the guilt and proclaim the guilt, in any and all, even ourselves. It is a mental attack machine. Its message to anyone, spoken or unspoken, is, "You screwed up. You're not good enough." Judgment, blame, and guilt are the ego's fuel.

The Holy Spirit, on the other hand, is the voice for love. It guides us to keep faith with the truth of God: that all of us are innocent because that is how He created us. This doesn't mean that what people do does not matter or that evil does not exist. It simply means that our task as miracle workers is to extend our perception beyond what our physical senses perceive, to what we know to be true in our hearts.*

When people do things that are not loving, it means they have lost contact with their true nature. They have fallen asleep to who they really are, dreaming the dream of an angry self or an arrogant self or a cruel self, and so forth. Our mission as miracle workers is to remain awake to the beauty in people even when they have forgotten it themselves. In that way, we subconsciously "re-mind" them who they are. As disciples of the Holy Spirit, we simultaneously see both the worldly error and the spiritual perfection in people. And in sharing God's perspective on human error—a desire to heal as opposed to a desire to punish—we become conduits of His healing power. Thus we too are healed.

To the ego, this is outrageous: how *dare* we declare the child of God innocent? Can't we *see* what a dark and sinful creature he is? Even religions that claim that God is good seem bent at times on finding His children guilty. Many point their fingers critically at other people, not realizing that the pointed finger itself is the source of all evil. It is the *concept* of enemy that is our greatest enemy of all.

What About Archie Bunker?

During one of my lectures once a man rose to ask a question. "I don't have a problem with anything you're saying," he said. "But my problem is what happens when I leave this room. What do we do about people who don't believe this way? Like my father; he's like Archie Bunker! What do I do about *him?*"

Many heads in the room started nodding, but I inwardly smiled. God doesn't let us get away with that one.

"Do you want to know?" I asked. "Do you really want to know what *A Course in Miracles* would say?"

He nodded.

"It would say you need to stop judging your father."

He and hundreds of others had a look on their faces as though to say, "Right, of course, I get it."

I continued. "Only what you are not giving can be lacking in any situation. God sent us here to work miracles, and we can only do that when we have given up our judgments. How can you help awaken your dad to his innocence if you yourself are stuck focusing on his guilt?

"And that's not to say it's always easy, either. But the primary responsibility of the miracle worker is to accept the atonement for *himself.* You're not here to monitor the spiritual progress of other people. The issues God wants us to address first are our own."

The miracle is not that his dad will become different but that he himself will become different. The irony, of course, is that he is probably judging his father for being judgmental! Only when he is no longer judging his dad, but accepting him as he is, are miracles possible.

I believe it was Martin Luther King Jr. who said that we have no morally persuasive power with someone who can feel our underlying contempt. Whose thoughts are we more likely to influence in a loving direction: someone who feels judged by us or someone who can see that all that love we *say* we believe in *applies to them as well?*

Eternal Perfection

Until we remember who we are, we are tempted to take on the shame and guilt of the ego. We see it in ourselves and project it onto others. We internalize the judgment and blame that are endemic to the world. I love the lyric from the Christmas carol "O Holy Night": "Long lay the world in sin and error pining, 'til He appeared and the soul felt its worth." If God's plan calls for us to remember our own eternal perfection, then wouldn't He be asking us to remember it in other people as well?

To the ego, the notion of eternal and unchangeable innocence is blasphemy. Guilt itself is the ego's god. But if we're to evolve beyond the ego, we have to evolve beyond our belief in the sanctity of guilt. And the place to begin is in regards to ourselves.

That doesn't mean we haven't made mistakes or that we don't need to try to make them right. But as it's often said, God's not finished with any of us yet. We're not perfect or we wouldn't have been born, but it's our mission to become perfect here.* One step at a time, one lesson after another, we're growing closer to the expression of our divine potential.

What is real is that you're a beloved child of God. You don't have to do anything to make that true; it's a Truth that was established in your creation. Your inherent perfection is a creation of God, and what God created can't be uncreated.*

Other people can think what they want to think about you, but it's only your own perceptions, not the projections of others, that program your future. It's when we *agree* with other people's projections that we get into trouble—when we give the ego power and align with its judgments. The ego is fueled by shame and loves to introduce it into any situation, directed toward ourselves or someone else; it doesn't really care. Yet we can learn to say no to shame, keeping our heads high and moving through life with the knowledge that all of us are equally blessed in God's eyes. We shouldn't have to apologize for the fact that each of us is an infinitely creative being, endowed by God with extraordinary potential that He would have us make manifest.

Sometimes we're ashamed because of something we actually did, but other times because of what other people just thought we did and seem intent on telling the world about. Either way, shame is one of the ego's most vicious weapons, sure to keep us stuck in patterns of guilt. And the purpose of the guilt is to keep us from the peace of God.

People who have the lives they want are people who have realized on some level that they deserve to have it. Many of our problems were called forth by the subconscious mind, a reflection of our own belief that on some level we deserve to be punished. That is the ego's constant message: "You are bad, you are bad, you are bad." And when the pain of that feeling gets too difficult to endure, we're tempted to think, "No, that person is bad, not me." One day we realize that there doesn't always have to be someone to blame. The terrible damage that is done in this world is less because of a few people whose hearts have actually turned to evil, and more because of the millions of basically good and decent souls whose hearts are wounded and left unhealed.

In any given moment, the universe is primed to give us new life, to begin again, to create new opportunities, to miraculously heal situations, to change all darkness to light and fear to love. God's light shines eternally clear, untarnished by our illusions. Our job is to take a deep breath, slow down, surrender all thoughts of past or future, and let the Holy Instant shine forth in our awareness. God is not daunted by our nightmares of guilt; He is ever awake to how beautiful we are. He made us that way, and so it is.

Self-Forgiveness

Sometimes you see negative patterns repeating themselves in your life and you don't know how to change them. You begin by recognizing that, as *A Course in Miracles* states, "I am not a victim of the world I see." Sometimes we can't *see* exactly how we created a disaster, but we can still take full responsibility for the fact that we did. And that is a beginning.

No matter what other people might have done to us—and there *are* people who are not nice in this world, who do terrible things—it is still our option to forgive, to rise above, to be defenseless, and also important to search our own minds and hearts for ways we might have helped create or attract their darkness. The fact that other people were bad in a situation doesn't necessarily mean you were all good.

It can be a difficult process to take that kind of brutally honest look at yourself. It can lead to painful self-condemnation, then a need for self-forgiveness that can be at least as hard as forgiving others.

Sometimes we realize some part of our personality is fear-based ego. Others might judge us for it, but that isn't even what's important. In fact, it is irrelevant because only someone's ego would feel the need to point out yours. Your ego issues don't matter because of other people's judgments of you; they matter because they are blocking your light, your joy, and your availability to God to use for His purposes. Sixty watts can't move through a thirty-watt bulb.

You're on this earth to shine your light for the sake of the entire world. The places in you where you are seemingly blocked in your ability to do that can be released to God for healing. Once you admit your defect and ask Him to take it away from you, His response to your invitation will be quick and sure. He remembers, even better than you do, the pain and suffering that led to your weakness. He was there for you when it happened, He cried tears as He watched you develop your dysfunction as a coping mechanism, and He rejoices at the invitation to heal you now.

Such are the miracles of God, and they will totally transform your life.

Whatever we refuse to look at in ourselves, we more easily project onto someone else. One of the benefits of facing our own weaknesses is that it helps us grow more compassionate toward others.

In any situation there is a focus to our perception. God would have us extend our perception beyond what the physical senses perceive, to the love that lies beyond. For when we see that love, we can *call it forth.* The physical senses reveal a veil of illusion: what people said and did on the mortal plane. But we lift the veil by seeing beyond it and invoking a truer truth. That is our purpose in each other's lives: to invoke each other's greatness and work a miracle in each other's lives.

According to *A Course in Miracles,* it's our job to tell someone they're right even when they're wrong.* That means we can affirm someone's essential innocence even when having to deal with their mistake. That distinction, however—between someone simply making a mistake you need to discuss with them and someone being "guilty" of something—is huge.

A conversation I had with a friend is an example.

My friend Ellen and I were doing a project together. A situation arose in which I was clear that I didn't want to take immediate action. She disagreed and kept pressuring me to do something.

I would say, "I don't want to do anything right now; I have to think about this," and she would come back with, "Why can't we just do it this way? Why not?"

Finally, feeling under pressure, I gave in to her. And of course, a few days later I realized I had made a mistake.

So here I was, annoyed with myself for having given in to pressure to do something that went against my own inner knowing and also annoyed at my friend for having pressured me in the first place. So the spiritual question was this: Should I say anything to her, or should I simply eat my feelings?

There is a middle way, in which we neither judge others nor suppress our feelings. We can express ourselves honestly and demonstrate compassion at the same time.

I shared with her that I wasn't happy about how I had been pressured into taking action. Ellen began to get defensive and say how much she loved me and that she would never have done that. I said, "Wait. I love you too. And I know you love me. But you *did* do that.

"It's a no-fault universe, Ellen. Our friendship is much, much bigger than a mistake that either of us made, and this situation doesn't touch the rock-bottom reality of our love for each other as friends. But *within* that love, friends have to be able to share their truth with each other. I need you to know that (1) I love you and this doesn't in any way change that, (2) I know I'm ultimately responsible for my own behavior, no matter what you did, and (3) I hope you will not pressure me like that again."

I could feel her relax, for she no longer felt the need to be defensive. And from then on, she did everything she could to rectify the problem. That one shift—from her fearing that her mistake was more important than our love to my clarity that our love was more important than her mistake—created an emotional opening that made all the difference. When we feel blamed, our defenses come up. And all defenses are a passive attack.* That cycle of emotional violence, however subtle, is the beginning of all conflicts in the world. Our shift made the difference between the situation hurting our relationship and deepening it. It did the latter because truth was present on every level.

Miracles occur when total communication is given and received.* Often we only communicate *half* the truth; we either stress our upset with someone without emphasizing the larger love surrounding the relationship, or we stress the love without honoring our need to talk about the problem. Either way is a nonmiraculous, uncreative use of the mind, and it will leave the heart unhealed.

God calls us to be both honest *and* compassionate. As He is.

Invoking the Good

Being caught in anger, judgment, and blame is disempowering; it throws us out of our center; it puts us at the effect of the love-lessness of someone else. To be there for a while is one thing; to stay there and try to justify it is wrong-minded and will not lead to peace. Spirituality challenges us to detach from the purely personal, emotional aspects of a situation—the ego's need to be right—in order to uplift ourselves to higher ground. That doesn't mean we don't feel our pain, our anger, our despair. But there is a way to *hold* such feelings in a sacred rather than chaotic way, so they heal us rather than poison us.

Whenever our lives aren't working the way we wish they would, our instinctive tendency is to blame someone else. From dysfunctional parents to corrupt society, bitter former spouses to disloyal colleagues, we carry with us a catalog of grievances: if only this or that were different, my life would be good. "I've been screwed, you see, and that's why I'm not happy."

Yet somewhere deep inside a little voice breaks through: "Maybe yes, maybe no . . ." The only way we can be happy is if we are willing to take responsibility for our own experience. Even when someone has truly wronged us, it is important to ask ourselves what part, however small, we might have unwittingly played in either creating the situation or at least allowing it to occur.

Our first work is to ask ourselves, "What did I do, or not do, to contribute to this disaster?" While others might have their own karma to clean up, we can at least try to clean up our own.

I had an experience that hurt me deeply, in which I found myself abused—not just by an individual, but by a group of people acting in a sort of psychological concert. My experience was not unique, as many people have experienced what I would call "institutional abuse."

Yet it was only when I was willing to withdraw my belief in the *ultimate reality* of what had been done to me that I could free myself from the *effects* of what had been done to me. On the level of spirit, no one had done anything to hurt me because on the level of spirit, only Love is real. Loveless behavior had certainly occurred, but if only love is real, then only love can touch me.* God could more than compensate for whatever damage had been done, for "what man intends for evil, God intends for good." As long as I held back my forgiveness, however, I held back my own healing as well.

If I could forgive what had happened to me, I would become deeper and more prepared to serve Him. It is none of my business what happens to others who were involved in this drama. The only drama that matters is the one in my own head and heart. If I can come to understand that no lies, no injustice, no transgression of any kind can begin to touch who I essentially am, then I will receive the greatest prize of all: I will *learn* who I essentially am. For the part of us that can be lied about, insulted, mistreated, or betrayed is only a fiction of our mortal mind. Marianne Williamson is a portion of a greater self, as we all are. I, Marianne Williamson, can be hurt, but the greater self in which I dwell cannot. Our opportunity, when in pain, is to remember that who we really are cannot be hurt. When we look beyond the mortal in our persecutor, we can then—and only then—experience that which is beyond the mortal in ourselves.

We can have a grievance or we can have a miracle; we cannot have both.* And I knew that I wanted a miracle. I did not want to carry any thoughts of malice or revenge. I wanted to be free of meanness shown to me, and perhaps I could do that only by rooting out any meanness within myself. If that was the lesson, I was willing to learn it. And the love I received during that time—from those who bore witness to my pain and did what they could to bring me comfort—made the cruelty of the situation bearable.

If we allow Him to, God compensates for such difficult times by using them to turn our lives into something even better than before. In the spiritual as well as the physical world, when the skies are darkest we get our best view of starlight. As the ancient Greek playwright Aeschylus wrote, "In our sleep, pain that cannot forget falls drop by drop upon the human heart and in our own despair, against our will, comes wisdom through the awful grace of God."

The Deepest Wrongs

Do you prefer to be right or to be happy?*

Clearly, people do terrible things sometimes. But if our focus is always on people's guilt, then we will find ourselves living in a dark and vicious universe. Our capacity to shift our focus from guilt to innocence is our capacity to change our world. This does not mean we should look away when bad things happen or cease the struggle for justice. It just means that there is a personal hook we don't have to sling ourselves onto—that we can always believe in the basic goodness of people even when their behavior does not reflect their goodness.

Contrary to popular opinion, this is neither a naive nor a weak position. It doesn't mean that we have illusions about the nature or the power of evil. Yet the miracle worker has a more, not a less, sophisticated view of how to deal with it. Did Gandhi never feel anger toward British imperialists? Did Martin Luther King Jr. never feel anger toward Southern bigots? Of course they did. They were human. Yet with the help of God they worked through their anger, moving past it to something much more powerful: the love that lay beyond. Their spiritual process informed their political and social process, giving them the ultimate authority to move hearts and thus move mountains.

Until we do that, we might get all kinds of people to agree with us in our position and support us in our anger. But in that way we will achieve short-term gains at best; we will not work miracles. Love is not just a feeling; it is a *force*. And it is a force that is ultimately more powerful than violence of any kind.

To forgive those who have transgressed against you is not to condone evil but rather to surrender it to a higher authority for ultimate justice. In the Bible it is said, "Vengeance is mine, sayeth the Lord." That means it's God's business, not yours. Even while prosecuting the worst crimes, we can remember that guilt in terms of humanly made law is not synonymous with guilt before God. When God parted the Red Sea in order for the Israelites to cross, the Egyptian soldiers then ran after them. At that point, God closed the waters, and the Egyptians drowned. When the Israelites began to rejoice at the destruction of their enemies, however, God commanded them to stop. They were not to rejoice at the death of other human beings, even when God's justice had deemed it necessary. So it is that we should never take pleasure in another's suffering, even if they "deserve" it. We are to hold to the light, to divine consciousness, even when we have to deal with the darkness of the world. Only in that way will the two one day be reconciled.

If you were completely victimized as the world defines it, then take heart from Dr. Martin Luther King Jr.'s notion that there is "redemptive power in unearned suffering." It's our spiritual assignment to love even those who have transgressed against us: for in the ultimate scheme of things, they are learning too.

The Miracle of Forgiveness

When I'm pondering how hard it can be to forgive, I'm reminded of people who have had infinitely more difficult things to forgive than I and who succeeded. They're like sacred role models, and the blessings they've called down upon themselves have blessed me as well.

One such inspirational example is Azim Khamisa. Azim's twenty-year-old son, Tariq, was a San Diego college student earning extra money delivering pizzas in the mid-1990s when he was gunned down by a fourteen-year-old boy in a senseless, gang-related homicide. Azim, like any parent of a murdered child, experienced trauma and grief beyond what seemed humanly endurable. Yet over the years he has demonstrated, and experienced, the miracle of forgiveness.

Azim, a religious Sufi, was told by his spiritual adviser that after forty days of grieving his son, he must turn his grief into good works. Only in that way, he was told, could he help his son move to the next stage of his soul's journey. Doing so then became Azim's mission in life: to act in such a way as to help his son even after he had died. He was told that instead of grieving the dead, he must do good, compassionate deeds for the living. For such deeds are like spiritual energy, providing high-octane fuel for the soul of the departed. In this way, Azim could serve his son although his son was no longer with him. Having felt that he had lost all reason to live, Azim came to feel new purpose in life. Channeling his grief into positive, meaningful work would benefit both Tariq and himself.

When Azim first heard that Tariq had been killed, he said it was as if "a nuclear bomb had gone off in my heart." He remembers the experience of leaving his body, and his life force, or *prana*, left with him. He went into the "loving arms of (his) maker," and when the explosion finally subsided, Azim came back into his body. When he returned, he had received a revelation: that there were victims on both sides of the gun.

That realization led Azim to reach out to the grandfather of the boy who killed his son, with whom the boy, Tony, had been living at the time of the murder. The grandfather, Ples Felix, was a Green Beret who had served two tours in Vietnam and had a master's degree in urban development. Tony had gone to live with his grandfather at the age of nine, after suffering frequent violent abuse himself as well as witnessing the murder of his cousin. By the time he was nine, Tony was already racked with anger. Reading in the papers about the boy and about his grandfather, Azim felt compassion for their story.

Azim asked the district attorney to introduce him to Ples, and they met in the office of the public defender who was representing Tony. Azim told Ples he felt no animosity toward Tony or his family, and he realized that both families had been traumatized by this tragic incident. He was concerned about Tony and all the other children who are trying to cope with such a violent world, in which the average American child has seen 100,000 images of violence on TV, movies, and video games before entering the first grade.

Azim told Ples he had started a foundation in the memory of his son, to help stop children from killing children. Ples said he would do whatever he could to help. As he extended his condolences, Ples told Azim that ever since the day of the murder, the Khamisa family had been in his daily prayers and meditations.

Azim invited Ples to the second meeting of the foundation a couple of weeks later, where Ples met the entire Khamisa family. Ples spoke passionately about his own experience, saying the foundation was an answer to his prayers. A San Diego television station filmed Tariq's grandfather shaking hands with Tony's grandfather: "Clearly," they reported, "this is a different kind of handshake."

Today, Azim is chairman of the Tariq Khamisa Foundation's board of directors, and Ples is the vice chairman. The men have grown close, and Azim says that if he were to choose ten people who are closest to him in his life, Ples would be one. The foundation has become a personal ministry for both men, and there is a job there waiting for Tony on the day he is released from prison.

The One That's Hard for All of Us

It's very difficult to talk or even think about forgiveness when confronted with the reality of September 11, 2001. Only silence—not words—can express the horror of that day.

Yet at the same time, a deeper conversation is available to us than the one now dominating our public dialogue. If we just hold to the simplistic line that "They're bad; we're good; let's kill 'em," then we're dangerously off base both spiritually and politically.

When the Twin Towers were first destroyed, the severity of the emotional blow threw America into our hearts. And with our hearts restored, our minds began working better as well. We were one nation, a true community, some of us experiencing it for the first time in our lives. And the very intelligent question on many people's lips was, "Why do those people hate us so much?" Over dinner tables and around office water coolers, we asked questions we had not been asking often enough over the last few decades: What has America been doing around the world, and how are we perceived by others? Even mainstream American television, not always known for its intellectual depth, hosted brilliant political thinkers and philosophers to educate the American people on issues we now painfully recognized were relevant to our lives.

Yet several days later it was like someone had pulled the plug. No more interesting thinkers on TV, just cheerleaders for revenge. We were to move into war mode, and quickly; that mode could not tolerate the suggestion that America had played even the tiniest part in attracting our misfortune. Anyone who even hinted such a thing was described as "blaming America." Clichés were substituted for meaningful conversation; intellectual excellence, healthy skepticism, and any discussion of spirituality or compassion as they related to the threat of terrorism were deemed the undermining machinations of unpatriotic Americans.

Yet I've noticed that it's the people who suffered the most on 9/11 who have often displayed the capacity for the highest vision of what occurred that day. From pushing for a 9/11 commission when the president himself was resisting it, to forming groups like September Eleventh Families for Peaceful Tomorrows which stand for compassion and forgiveness in the midst of this haunting darkness, those who suffered the most have taken the strongest stand for the power of truth.

One day I was watching a TV roundtable discussion with three victims of 9/11. One woman had lost her husband at the World Trade Center; one man had lost his young son, who was working at the Pentagon when it was bombed. At the end of the discussion, the news anchor asked one last question: "Do you want revenge?"

A pained expression crossed the face of each member of the roundtable at that question. I remember the woman saying, "No, because I can't imagine anyone else having to go through the pain we've been through." The man who lost his son said, "No, I think we've got to find a way to make those people over there know who we really are so they won't hate us anymore." The third panelist said something similar. And then the TV journalist, who himself had suffered no personal loss on 9/11, said this: "Well, *I* want revenge, and I want it to be fierce and swift." It was obvious that those who had suffered the most had been lifted up to a place that he had not. They didn't want to continue the violence; they just wanted the violence to end.

There are wars that the vast majority of us would call "righteous wars," such as America's involvement in World War II. Now, as then, there are people who wish our country harm and would kill us if they could; it is clearly both our right and our responsibility to defend ourselves. But the conversation should not stop there. If our first responsibility as individuals is to accept the atonement for ourselves, then America's first order of business should be getting our own actions right with God. No nation should fear deep reflection and self-examination. What we should fear is our urge to avoid them.

America has our own atonement to attend to. A humble heart, through which we admit our own errors and seek to live in more righteous relationship with the peoples of the world, is a spiritual approach to our current situation that is a healthy complement to more aggressive problem-solving options. As long as brute force is deemed the greatest power and love is deemed essentially weak, then we are mocking God and dealing dangerously with our future.

Not every cancer can be surgically removed, and when it is inoperable, we now know that spiritual practice can be efficacious in helping to heal the body. Terrorism is not an operable tumor, though perhaps we're pretending that it is. It is in fact a cancer that has already metastasized throughout the global body, and while some invasive measures might be appropriate, a holistic perspective—in which we recognize the powers of the mind and heart to help activate our social immune system—brings a more mature and effective means of dealing with it than the ego's sole reliance on retribution and revenge. If hate is more powerful than love, then we're on the right track. If love is more powerful than hate, then we're headed in a very, very wrong direction.

At the center of the American ideal are eternal values of justice and right relationship. The only way to navigate these somewhat dangerous times is to cleave to our values, not turn away from them in pursuit of short-term advantage. Nations, like individuals, emerge spiritually from the Mind of God. We will only find our safety in Him, and He is love.

In Him, we are all one. He loves every nation as much as He loves ours, and the blessing of the United States has been our stand for the equality of all people. In turning away from that stand—in building so many barriers between ourselves and others—we are literally spurning God. His greatest gift to us is not that He will give us victory in battle, but that He will lift us above the battlefield.* From there, we will see what we are not seeing now. And the power of that vision will pave the way to true peace.

CHAPTER EIGHT

From *Separation* to *Relationship*

*E*ach of us is the center of the universe. Everything we experience is happening inside us, not outside. At the deepest level, *there is no world outside us.** The world as we know it is a manifest projection of our thought forms, no more and no less. It is thought up, and it is thought up by each of us.

We are slavishly devoted to the ego's notion that we're our bodies—mere tiny specks of dust surrounded by a huge universe over which we have no control. And if that's what we think, then that will be our experience. But there is another way of viewing the world, through which we recognize that our life force is limitless because we are one with an unlimited God. No matter what we do or what we have done, now, in this moment, we are temples embodying the glory of God. Any situation seen through the light of this understanding is miraculously transformed.

Close your eyes and imagine yourself as you appear in the world. And now see a golden light that radiates from your heart, extends beyond your body, and casts a light to the entire world. Now imagine someone else standing next to you, friend or foe, and see the same light within that person. Watch the light as it grows to cover his or her body and extends beyond it. Now see the light in the other person as it merges with the light in you. On the level of spirit, there is no place where others stop and you start.

If you do this with anyone, your relationship with that person will subtly change. In the Christmas carol where we sing, "Do you see what I see?" there is a deeper question being asked than whether someone sees a physical child in a manger. "Do you see what I see?" refers to a question of consciousness, as in, do you see that spiritual reality? Do you grasp it, can you imagine it? For if you do, you can have it. The possibility exists.

When we realize we're not who we think we are—that the world has taught us a huge and unholy lie—we realize that other people aren't who *they* appear to be either. And neither are our relationships, for as spirits we are not separate, but one.

An idea does not leave its source.* You are literally an idea in the mind of God, which is why you cannot be separate from Him. And the world you experience is an idea in your mind, which is why it can't be separate from you.

We're like sunbeams thinking we're separate from the sun or waves thinking we're separate from the ocean.* But sunbeams can't *be* separate, and waves can't *be* separate of course.* The idea of our separation is nothing but a vast hallucination.* And yet that's where we live: in the illusion that you're over there and I'm over here. That illusion—that we are separate—is the source of all our pain.

The ego suggests that that space will be filled by one "special" person, rather than by a corrected sense of our relationship to everyone. Yet that is a lie. Just think about it: if in fact you're one with everybody yet you think you're not, then imagine how many people you subconsciously miss being with! No wonder we feel such a hole, such an existential emptiness inside us. What we miss is a right-minded relationship with everyone.

Feeling separate from love, we feel a panic so deep we don't even recognize it. Just as the earth is moving so fast we can't feel the speed anymore, our hysteria is so deep we don't hear our own scream anymore. Yet it permeates our being, demanding we do something, anything, to assuage the pain. And God knows we try: in ways both healthy and unhealthy, we keep trying to fill the hole that only surrendering to our love for all of life can fill. And always, there is the anger that the separation engenders: our anger at feeling separate, although we're not consciously aware from what.

In God there is escape, for He has sent the Holy Spirit to reunite our hearts by correcting our thinking. He can dismantle our thought system based on fear and replace it with a thought system based on love. He will give us a new mind.

This new mind awaits us in this next stage of our evolutionary journey. We are being challenged by the forces of history to grow into this mind, to mutate, as it were, in order for our species to survive. Jesus had the new mind, called in him the Christ Mind, as did Buddha and others. It is the mind when it is overshadowed by God, our mind when it has become one with His, when we have touched the heavenly light and been permanently altered by it. This state of enlightenment is the exaltation of our existence, the uplifting of our human consciousness to such a high place that we manifest, at last, as the children of God we truly are.

And when we do—when we realize that we are not just *like* each other, but we actually *are* each other—then we will begin to find life outside the realm of love no longer acceptable. In time, it will become literally unthinkable. And becoming unthinkable, *it will cease to exist.*

Melting the Walls

How many times have you seen a pattern in your relationships you felt powerless to change? How often have you despaired of ever breaking free of self-sabotaging behavior? How deeply have you panicked at the thought that you might never get it right?

Our despair and panic are natural responses to the relationship dramas we create in our lives. But our tears are not what we think they are because the predicament itself is not what we think it is. What separates us from others is not just codependency or neediness or any other mere psychological issue. Our barriers to love represent a cosmic force, ensconced within the human psyche in a dark and insidious way, holding dominion—temporary though wicked—over the mental functioning of the child of God. It is completely irrelevant what form the barrier takes. Our concentration on the form of fear is an ego ploy to keep us stuck in the problem, like finding a thief in your house and saying, "I have to know his name before I call the police." Who cares what his name is? Call for help immediately!

The ego is our deepest enemy masquerading as our closest friend. It is nothing we should fear, however, because the moment we recognize it as merely a mental miscreation—simply a false belief about who we are—it will disappear into the nothingness from whence it came. We ourselves, however, cannot command its departure. It has absconded with our will and confused our defenses. Like an immune system disease that attacks its own cells, the ego attacks the mind it purports to give life to. Only God can help us.

And He will. He will show us the innocence in others, that we might see it in ourselves. Through His Holy Spirit He will outwit our self-hatred and return our hearts to love.*

Most of us—all of us, in fact, except the enlightened masters—live to some extent in a state of "love withhold." We are waiting to see if a person is good enough to receive our kindness, our generosity, or our love. People hardly have dates anymore; we have *auditions*. We think we need to understand a person to see whether they are worthy of our love, but in fact, unless we love them we cannot understand them.*

Someone's religion, looks, financial status, professional position—so many things are used by the ego to dictate who is worthy or appropriate for us. Yet God would have us keep our hearts open to people as a matter of faith. And any faith that has us close our hearts to anyone is not a genuine faith in God.

God is not outside us, nor is He outside our relationship to each other. Relationships are the contesting ground between ego and spirit, which begins developing as soon as we are born.

All of us were born with a completely open heart, making no distinction between who deserves our love or not. Yet the experience of a fearful world—in which it is sad but necessary to teach our children that there are dangers of which they indeed must beware—has trained us to shut down the emotional valve from which otherwise pours forth universal compassion. Love, which is our very nature, begins to feel unnatural, and fear begins to feel natural.* Once we have lived long enough, a closed heart rather than an open one becomes our instinctive response to life.

And sometimes this happens much sooner than it should. One evening I went out with my elderly mother to a lovely restaurant, and after dinner we went to the women's room. As my mother was washing her hands, a little four- or five-year-old girl came up to the sink next to her. My mother, who grew up in what I think was in many ways a more civilized era, went over to the little girl as she struggled to reach the faucet and said, "Here, honey, I'll help you!"

At that moment, the child's mother came out of her stall, saw my mother, practically knocked her out of the way, and gave her the meanest glance you can imagine. The look of hurt on my mother's face was painful to witness. I thought to myself, "What you are teaching your daughter by making her completely distrust everyone she ever meets is more risky than the risks you are seeking to protect her from." I have a daughter, and of course I've had to teach her never to go anywhere with strangers, and so on. But not talk to them? Or be nice to them? Or be open in any way? Is that the world we want to create?

The ego would propose a world in which no one ever receives a smile unless they "earn" it. And is that where we desire to live? The love and beneficence we show each other on a daily basis— in the grocery store, standing in line at the bank, walking down the street—can be as important as any grand gesture we show to a so-called loved one. To God, we are all loved ones. And when we learn to love each other as He loves us all, we will prepare the table for the love we most want.

Even When It's Hard

One day I was thinking about my need to love the people I disagree with politically. This has been particularly difficult for me in the last few years, as it has been for many people. I was asking God to show me the innocence in some people that I couldn't quite see for myself.

In my meditation I had a vision. In it, I witnessed a terrible car accident. I was the first person to arrive on the scene, where I saw that a man was trapped in the car and the car was about to catch on fire. I immediately did everything possible to save him; all that mattered was that someone's life was in danger. I passionately worked, clawed, struggled—and ultimately succeeded. After a huge and prolonged effort, I finally freed the man and dragged him out of the car. And when I saw his face, I realized he was—Donald Rumsfeld!

So that was it. The message couldn't have been plainer. Every human being is first and foremost just that—another human being—and if I can see them that way, then I will be free. I might still disagree with people, even work for their political retirement perhaps, but I will be free of the emotional entanglements that judgment breeds. Everyone, no matter who, is a child of God. And until I get that, I'm not where I need to be to help change our damaged world. In fact, I'm just adding my own damage to it.

If I look at my judgments of you and simply lay them aside as the work of the ego, *which I do not have to obey*—then I am contributing to the work of peace on earth. And only if I am willing to give up my own judgments do I have the right to call myself a peacemaker. This is much harder than traditional peace activism because it means we're seeking the deepest change within ourselves.

The judgmental mind is a problem, then, isn't it? It's the voice that says, "You can love this one but not that one." Our job is to learn to love as God loves, which means everyone all the time. That is not to say *like* everyone; it is not to say date or marry everyone; it is not to say have lunch with everyone. It is not even to say trust everyone, on the level of personality. The love that will save us is an impersonal, not a personal love—a love that is unconditional because it's based not on what people do but on who they essentially are.

Trust

Then what are we to do about people who are genuinely not to be trusted? Are we supposed to just love people, even when they take advantage of us? At what point do we set up defenses and boundaries, keeping unsafe people at bay?

A while ago, I found out that a close associate—who at the time I thought was also a close friend—had embezzled a large amount of money from me. One week after we finally came up with a legal solution, a few former friends and associates perpetrated a vicious and dishonest campaign to undermine my work. Obviously, I was devastated. What had I done to attract such unscrupulous people? And how had I contributed to their betrayal?

Pondering the spiritual meaning of these situations, my main question regarded trust. I had trusted these people; I had expected them to behave decently. Was the lesson to be learned that I was not to trust?

Then I realized that I needed to be more trustworthy toward myself. No one could have stolen so much money if I had kept better track of it myself, and I should not have still been dealing with people who many times before had demonstrated their lack of ethical standards. In both those situations, there were ways in which I should have known better. I was blinded to what I *knew* to be true because of what I *wanted* to be true. I wasn't listening deeply to my own inner knowing, and even when its voice broke through, I didn't heed it when I didn't want to. Thus I suffered, but I also learned.

In a way, I came out of those situations not trusting people less so much as trusting myself more. I think those circumstances were important lessons for me—in choosing associates more wisely, in being more responsible toward myself, and of course in discerning between the perfection of the soul and the pernicious potential in every personality. I have now experienced other people's viciousness, as many of us have. But until I have removed every bit of it from myself, I am not a victim. I am simply standing in front of a very big mirror and seeing myself as I grow through my stuff. All that is not love is a call for love, and every situation is an opportunity to grow.

Relationships Are Laboratories

Relationships are laboratories of the Holy Spirit, but they can also be playgrounds for the ego. They can be heaven, or they can be hell. They are infused with love or infused with fear.

Most of the time, they are a little of both.

The ego speaks first and the ego speaks loudest, and it will always make a case for separation: the other peron did this or that and therefore does not deserve our love.* And in whatever moment we choose to listen to the ego—denying love to someone else—then to that extent we will be denied. Knowing that the mind works that way, we can call for help. We can pray for a power greater than our own to push back the storm of neurotic thinking.

To the ego, the purpose of a relationship is to serve our needs as we define them. *I want to get this job; I want him or her to marry me; I want this person to see things the way I do.* To the Holy Spirit, the purpose of a relationship is to serve God.

Every relationship is part of a divine curriculum designed by the Holy Spirit. It is there for a reason, but the reason might not be the one we ascribe to it. The ego and God have diametrically opposed intentions.

The only way to make sure we're not playing sick and destructive mind games in a situation—particularly in relationships where the ego has so much invested—is to invite the Holy Spirit to enter there and prevail. At the earliest moment you think to do it, place a relationship on the altar to God within your mind.

Dear God,
I place my relationship with . . .
In Your hands.
May my presence be a blessing in his life.
May my thoughts toward him be those of innocence and love,
And may his thoughts toward me be those of innocence and love.
May all else be cast out.
May our relationship be lifted
To divine right order,
And take the form
That best serves Your purposes.
May all unfold,
In this and all things,
According to Your will.
Amen.

From Woundedness to Healing

Sometimes we try to take the paintbrush out of God's hands, under the erroneous assumption we can paint a better picture than He can. The ego will try to get a relationship to fit into our idea of how it should be rather than allowing it to organically reveal itself. We have pictures and idealizations we try to foist on others, thinking, "It should feel like this," or "They should act like that." Yet at the deepest level, we are simply souls encountering other souls, and relationships should be places where we free each other, not imprison each other. When our consciousness is simply that of one child of God honoring another—regardless of how things look in the outer world—we exude a peace and acceptance that calls people to their highest. When we're calm, people around us will be calmer; when we're kind, people around us will be kinder; when we're peaceful, people around us will be more peaceful. Once we find the love within ourselves, calling it forth in our relationships comes much more easily.

Yet even when relationships are good, the ego is always alert to ways it can drive two hearts apart. The ego directs us toward love but then sabotages it once it gets here. You think you're so in love, but then you act needy and repel it. You think you're feeling peaceful, but then love comes near and you get totally neurotic. You want to make a good impression, and then you go and act like an idiot.

The ego is always on the lookout for ways to undermine our relationships because genuine relationship means death to the ego. Where we unite with another, God *is;* and where God is, ego cannot be. To the ego, therefore, undermining our relationships is an act of self-preservation. The only way to ward off its destructiveness is to stand firm in your commitment to love—not just as a commitment to another person, who to the ego may or may not "deserve" it—but as a commitment to God and to yourself.

Loving thoughts can become a mental habit. Sometimes, when we're impatient with each other, it helps to think of the person we're dealing with as they must have been like as a child. For all of us are children in God's eyes. When children are young we know they're growing, and we take this into account in our dealings with them. We don't expect a twelve-year-old to have the maturity she or he will have at eighteen.

And as adults we're still growing too, whether or not we can always see that in each other. We're not finished once we reach a certain age; rather, we continue to grow and develop as long as we're alive. We learn, as children do. We stumble, as children do. And we sometimes fail, as children do. God sees all of us that way, no matter how old we are. He has infinite mercy upon us, and we could have mercy too.

None of us arrives in any relationship already healed, already perfect. In a holy relationship, it is understood we are all wounded but we are there to be healed together.* When the relationship is seen as a temple of healing, with mutual and proactive beneficence our daily medicine, the ego will then have far less power to snatch away our joy.

Categories of Love

There is no love but God's.*

To the ego there are different categories of love—between parent and child, between friends, between lovers, and so forth. But those categories are made up by us: in God, there is but one love. In every relationship, the fundamental things apply.

When my daughter was a little girl, I was surprised at times by how sophisticated her perceptions were. Once I said something slightly teasing about a book she was reading, and she responded by making it clear to me she felt my comments were disrespectful. And she was right; the fact that she was nine years old didn't mean she didn't have a right to her tastes and her opinions and her feelings. (Now that she's a teenager, of course, I get to remind her that I do too!)

A little respect, a little honor, can go a long way. Sometimes it's not the broad philosophic issue of cosmic innocence versus worldly guilt, but the simple ways we communicate to one another that determine whether love or fear pervades a relationship.

Someone who was working for me once said she was about to call the manager of the hotel where I had lectured the day before.

"Why?" I asked.

"I need to tell him about all the mistakes they made on Sunday."

"Whoa," I said. "Let's not do that!"

"What do you mean?" she said. "Remember all the things they forgot to take care of—the parking, the piano, the signs?"

"Sure, I remember," I said. "But this is what I've learned: if you approach that phone call just telling them what they did wrong, then that's not going to ultimately get us anywhere. They might acquiesce to our complaints, but they'll be feeling offended and hurt, and that hurt will show up in other ways down the line. When people aren't allowed to be directly aggressive, they often become passively aggressive. If people resent you, they will find a way to show it.

"So let's try another way. Didn't they do a lot of things right?"

"Sure," she said.

I continued. "I mean, the room was beautiful, the sound was great, they provided lovely refreshments, they created a homey atmosphere—they tried really hard to make us all feel welcome. Isn't that true?"

"Okay, I'll let Alex make the call. She's always really nice about things like that."

"No, Maggie," I said. "This is about more than just being nice. I'm not just talking about behavior modification; I'm talking about transformation. I'm talking about surrendering our need to focus on someone's guilt. If anyone on our team is thinking thoughts like that, it affects the whole team.

"We are all responsible not just for our behavior but for our attitudes, because our attitudes affect a situation as much as our behavior does. Everything we do, including—sometimes especially!—work, is a journey of transformation."

Later that afternoon I heard Maggie on the phone with the manager of the hotel. "Hey, I want to thank you for all the things you guys did to make it so great on Sunday!" she began. I heard them chatting nicely for the next couple of minutes. And then I heard her say, in a very kind voice, "Hey, I was wondering if I could go over a couple of things with you." She proceeded to mention, in polite and understanding ways, the issues that still needed to be addressed.

And they were.

I've had situations in my life where someone had a problem with something I'd said, and in looking back I exclaimed, "But I was right! I said the right thing!" And then I've gotten back the proverbial response: "It wasn't what you said; it was how you said it." A tone of voice can heal, and a tone of voice can hurt.

What the ego doesn't want us to realize is the practicality of love. We receive the experience of compassion to the extent to which we extend the experience of compassion. And you never know where it's most important.

Martha Stewart had her entire life brought to the brink of disaster by, as much as anything else, her personal manners. The fact that she offended her *broker's assistant* would come to affect her entire life. Here is a woman whose prodigious talents make the average person's lifetime achievements look paltry, yet she was stymied by her own personality issues. No amount of money, no professional achievements, and no external power can totally compensate for lack of people skills. At the deepest level, our relationships and personal issues define our lives.

Behind every problem is a broken relationship. And behind every miracle, there is a healed one.

Turning Issues into Miracles

Every relationship is a teaching-learning assignment. Anyone we are destined to meet, we will. We are drawn to each other for teaching and learning, as each of us is presented with the chance to learn the next lesson in the journey of our soul. Every encounter is a holy encounter if we use it to demonstrate love.* And every encounter is a setup for possible pain if we're not open to the opportunity to do that. Anyone we meet we were destined to meet, but what we do with the relationship is entirely up to us.

Sometimes someone is brought into our life to help us learn a lesson we've failed to learn before: to be accepting rather than controlling, to be approving instead of critical, or even to turn away from toxic behavior when before we would have made a beeline for it. It's no accident that certain patterns plague us, year after year, until we finally heal them. There's no point trying to go to Outer Mongolia to escape your issues; they will find you there because they live inside your head. The people you need will be brought to you; you will subconsciously attract them; there is no escaping the curriculum of the Holy Spirit.

If we have a particular problem in relationships, then we'll encounter that issue again until it's resolved. It represents a place where we become unconscious, unable to live in the fullness of our being. At that place, we break off into a fragment of ourselves, an impostor who puts a mask in front of our true face. We're lost there, not recognizing the alien environment we've created; we start grasping for emotional air, not knowing that we ourselves are the ones depriving us. This, to be sure, is the meaning of hell.

It is extremely difficult, in such moments, to use mere self-will to change ourselves. Yet if we ask for a miracle, we will receive one. For God is as clear in the Holy Instant as we would have Him be.* His mind, joined with our mind, can shine away the ego.* When lost in our illusions, His Spirit is there to bring us back.

Yet we can't just pray and meditate and expect all our personality issues to resolve themselves without any effort on our part. We have to use our prayer and meditation time to consciously *release* our relationship issues to God, that there they might be transformed. Our darkness must be brought to the light; it can't just be covered over by the light.

It's interesting to note the differences between a traditional psychotherapeutic approach to such issues and a more spiritual one. In most psychotherapy, the focus is put on the personality weakness and how to solve it. Why do we act this way? What childhood experience led to this problem? And sometimes that discussion can be very helpful. But when a more spiritual dimension is introduced to the psychotherapeutic process, we not only focus on the problem, we also pray for a divine answer.

Where our personalities are weak, we are stymied in our ability to manifest the glory of our true selves. Looking for who or what shut us down can be like looking back at the shore you just came from when you're lost in the river and can't find your way across. Better you should look toward the place you're heading (like Jesus or Buddha) and ask for guidance in crossing over. When we focus on perfection, our mind begins to head that way. We outgrow the ego as we grow closer to God.

Every time we have a problem in a relationship, we will repeat it unless we learn what we need to learn from it. This learning is part of the Atonement process, as we admit to God the mistakes we now realize we've made and pray for His help in changing us. We pray as well that He help heal whatever damage we might have done already, in our own lives or in someone else's.

Sometimes, when we have erred, there is nothing we can specifically do to make things better; it wouldn't help to make a call, send an e-mail, or whatever. But what we can change is our thinking, and the rest will follow. We might have to wait until a situation comes around again, either in this relationship or in another, and take advantage of the opportunity to act differently next time. As we do, the new behavioral pattern becomes embedded in our psychic repertoire. In time, it replaces the old.

When gemologists want to smooth out a rough sapphire or emerald, they do it by rubbing two stones up against each other. And that's often how relationships are: your rough edges rub against mine, and finally, after we suffer enough, we smooth out.

Romantic Delusions

Nowhere do we have more illusionary ideas of what love means than in the area of romance. We're trained by a world of cultural imagery to believe there is someone, one special someone, who will complete us and make us whole.

Yet what will make us whole is a deeper love for everyone. Exclusive love is not the prize it purports to be, and in truth, romantic love works far, far better when it is grounded in a larger, more inclusive love. Romance is one form that love takes—certainly a magnificent one—and yet it is content, not form, that determines love's meaning. If we are attached to that particular form of love, then we are on a slippery slope toward the fires of hell. And what are those fires? They are the anxiety we feel when that person doesn't call or acts in a way we interpret as unloving or doesn't want us anymore.

One of the biggest mistakes we make in relationships is when we get a fixed notion of what love should look like. If he loves me, he will do this. If she wants to be my friend, she will do that. But what if the feelings we want the other person to have simply don't express themselves the way we think they should? Are we going to forgo a love because it doesn't come in the package we expected it to arrive in? Relationships aren't black and white, and people aren't good or bad. We're complicated. We're trying our best. The more we live, the more we realize that the failure of others to love us the way we wish they would is as unintentional as our own such failures. Who among us isn't doing the best we're capable of, with the understanding we've got?

The ego argues that the right intimate relationship would take away all the pain of separation, yet that is delusional. Intimacy isn't a special category so much as a deeper layer of existence. When we first hold a baby in our arms, that is an intimate moment. When we sit with someone when they die, that is an intimate moment. When we share deeply from our core about our genuine feelings, that is an intimate moment. Our obsession with romantic love as the primary container for intimacy has often kept us from finding it. It is two hearts—not two bodies—that make a holy connection. When the body comes along, that's fantastic. But anyone with any experience knows that sex itself doesn't guarantee deep connection. And at times, it can obstruct it.

A Course in Miracles teaches the difference between "special" love and "holy" love. "Special" love means we are attached to another person being a certain way. We think we know what we need from a person and put our focus on trying to make it happen. Not realizing we are looking to a human relationship to fill a space that only God can fill, we are willing to go to extraordinary lengths to make the other person, or ourselves, fit into the picture our ego thinks is perfect.

The problem with this is that control and manipulation, however subtle, are not love. Love is repelled by any effort to hold onto it too tightly. God's response to the ego's "special" relationship is the creation of the "holy" relationship, in which we allow a relationship to be what it wants to be and reveal its meaning to us rather than trying to determine its meaning first.

"Holy" love allows another person to simply be who he or she is. It helps us detach from the need to control another person's behavior. Yet all of that is much easier said than done. Holy love is a pretty awesome goal for those of us stuck in our bodies in an imperfect world. Are we not to have any expectations in relationship? While it is the body that ties us to the material realm, that realm is where we are living. And we have appropriate and valid needs here.

I had an interesting lesson in nonattached love when I moved into a house with a male roommate. He's a fun person who loves excitement, traveling here and there, going off on his motorcycle. He's available when he's home, but don't even try to get him on his cell phone when he's elsewhere. I once said to him, "Casey, I understand you don't listen to your phone messages very often. But what would happen if the house burned down?"

He responded, "I guess I'd come home to a lot of ashes!"

I can appreciate Casey, even chuckle at his antics and be entertained by his dramatic entrances and exits, for one main reason: that we don't have a physical relationship. For the ego uses the body to bind us to perceptions of need and control. Whenever we're identifying with the life of the body as opposed to the life of the spirit, then the ego is in charge.

I once asked him, "But what if we were involved romantically? Your behavior would drive me nuts!" To which he responded, "If we were involved romantically, I wouldn't act this way!" That's reasonable and hopefully true, for the sake of the women in his life. But I don't know. Sex and detachment are a difficult mix and the greatest challenge within romantic love.

Several months ago I had dinner with a man I once dated but had not seen in years. The subject of politics came up, and neither of us had moved too far to the left or to the right over the last decade. We were at opposite ends of the political spectrum then, and we are at opposite ends now. What has changed, however, is that we aren't trying to change each other anymore.

We were already well into the meal when I said to him, "You realize that if this were ten years ago, both of us would be covered with scratch marks by the time the salad came!" We were saying the same things we used to say, with just as much conviction, but neither of us was reacting the same way anymore. It had finally dawned on us that other people could have different opinions, and dinner could still be good!

I remember, when I was a child, how different the reading material piled up next to my father's side of the bed was from the reading material piled up next to my mother's side of the bed. He read Goethe and Aristotle; she read Judith Krantz and Belva Plain. It never seemed odd to them that they read such different things, but I grew into an adult who wouldn't hesitate to ask, "Why are you reading *that?*" To which a man once responded to me with a sweet smile and a fabulous kiss, and then said, "None of your goddamn business!"

When I see a woman trying to control a man, even slightly, I think to myself, "Honey, it might work for you, but it sure never worked for me!"

What I've learned is that it's okay to set agreements and to share my feelings, as long as I refrain from judgment and blame. From that place—as long as I avoid the temptation to try to steer another person's behavior—miracles do occur. It's amazing how positively people respond when they feel respected for their thoughts and feelings. Learning to feel such respect—and to actually *show* it—is key to a miracle worker's power.

Levels of Teaching

There are three levels of relationship "teaching assignments."* The first is what we would consider a casual encounter, in which it doesn't seem like anything is really happening at all.* A child accidentally drops a ball in front of us, or we share an elevator with someone. Will we throw the ball back to the child in a friendly manner, or smile at the person in the elevator? These supposedly accidental encounters are not accidental at all.*

The second level of teaching occurs when we are brought together with someone for a fairly intense learning experience, perhaps for weeks or months or years.* And we will stay together as long as physical proximity serves the highest learning opportunity for both people.*

The third level of teaching involves a "lifelong assignment";* this could be a friend, a relative, a love with whom our relationship lasts a lifetime. Sometimes it's a joyful assignment, like a brilliant lifelong love affair. And sometimes it's a painful one—relatives who cause each other grief throughout their lives. Whatever it is, however, it's part of a curriculum designed by the Holy Spirit.

Once we are joined in genuine relationship, it is never over. Whom God hath put together, no one and nothing can put asunder. While a particular form of relationship might change—through separation or through death—a relationship is never over because a relationship is of the spirit, and spirit is eternal. We are in physical connection for as long a period of time as serves the highest learning opportunity for both people, and then we merely appear to separate.* The love lives on because love cannot die.

When Yoko Ono was asked how she could bear being without John Lennon given that they had spent 90 percent of their time together, her response was, "Now we spend 100 percent of our time together." The death of the body is not the death of love.

The above is not a glib concept; it doesn't mean we don't cry, feel hurt, or grieve the loss of a love. But it does mean we have a context for transcending the loss. When our hearts remain open to the flow of Truth, the spirit can compensate for material loss. This is what happens, for instance, when people move through a divorce with loving intention, praying for God's healing of all hearts involved. Divorce is a spiritual issue with profound emotional consequences. How many children have been damaged by bitterly divorced parents? How many adults have been wounded for years, or even a lifetime, not realizing the eternal nature of a love they think they permanently lost? In delivering a divorce into the hands of God, we are asking that the relationship remain blessed in spirit though dissolved in body.

All who meet will someday meet again until their relationship becomes holy.* Whether we meet again in this lifetime or not, those who meet and love are tied together in eternity. Through the grace of God, we shall be reconciled one day. If we ever loved someone, we found them first in heaven. And it is to heaven that we will return.

Form versus Content

Someone once sent me a photograph that had been taken by a fisherman in Newfoundland. It was a picture of an iceberg, not only the part of it that protrudes above the water line, but also what's underneath the water. We all know, of course, that what is visible on top of the water is approximately 10 percent of the iceberg. Still, seeing the image was mind-blowing. It's shocking to recognize how much of life our eyes don't see.

And every situation is like that iceberg, teeming with forces that aren't visible to the physical eye. Basing our sense of reality on what the physical senses perceive as real—what people did, what people said—we base our sense of reality on a small fraction of its entirety. This means, of course, that we're hardly in touch with reality at all.

What is visible to the physical eye is the world of form, while the greater reality of a situation is not its form but its content.* Marriage is form, while love is content; age is form, while spirit is content. The only eternal reality lies in the realm of content, and content never changes. Our spiritual power lies in navigating a changing world from the perspective of that which does not change. The more we know about what's below the waterline, the more power we have above it.

We think if this or that happens in the world of form, then our lives will be fine. But while we habitually look to the material realm for something to complete us, our actual completion lies in knowing that the material realm itself is just one aspect of our greater life.

Living in the realm of body identification rather than spirit identification, we are constantly at risk for the experience of loss. We think we lose every time something in the world of form doesn't unfold the way we wish it to. Let's say I am in love with a man, we're together for a while, but then one of us decides the romantic attachment isn't working. To the ego, that means the relationship is over; to the spirit, that means the relationship simply changes form. And the spirit is correct. As much as a situation like that can bruise the heart, a higher vision of what really occurred can heal us. Love is eternal content, and it is safe and secure in the hands of God.

When We Grieve

Grief is an important healing mechanism, a way the psyche makes the transition from one situation to another. Our contemporary mania for pulling ourselves up by the bootstraps, getting back to work as soon as possible after a deep loss, and staying active no matter what is not always a perfect antidote to pain. In our modern bias for "feeling good," we often make ourselves wrong for feeling bad. Yet grief is a bad feeling without which we can never get back to the good ones.

Once I was grieving a painful situation in my life. Six weeks after the event, while talking to a friend about it, another friend walked out of the room saying, "I'm leaving. You guys can continue to obsess about this." I said, "Susan, a year from now, you can call it obsessing. After six weeks, it's still called processing." While we often bemoan the fact that people don't feel their emotions deeply enough, we're still tempted to blame them when they do.

And so, instead of allowing ourselves to grieve, we often force ourselves to suppress the grief, mistaking it for negativity or self-indulgence. Yet it is dangerous to shut out or suppress our pain because events we don't process we are doomed to repeat, or at least act out in dysfunctional ways. The time to cry is when we need to cry. Only then will we ultimately not need to cry anymore.

When a relationship is over, whether through separation or death, our center of emotional gravity shifts. We view life from a different spot on the mountain when someone who used to be next to us is no longer there. It is a good idea to do a thirty-day prayer vigil for the person who is no longer physically present with us, whether our conscious feelings for that person are loving or not. Prayer will neutralize the feelings, lifting them to serenity and peace. Going out shopping will not do this; dating or getting married again as fast as possible will not do this. Only being with yourself, your loved ones, and God will do this. You will internalize the change, your internal scars will heal, and you will, you will, be better than before.

The Spaces in Between

There is a mystery to the spaces in between relationships, when we have the opportunity to understand more deeply, to correct our course, and to redirect our ship if necessary. When a relationship is over, we can look back at it honestly, assess our part in it, and forgive ourselves and others if necessary. Did I or did I not show up for the relationship as authentically and honorably as I might have? Was I in it for the right reasons? Did I stay too long? Did I leave too quickly? Did I allow God to guide its course?

It can be helpful to make a list of every person and situation associated with the situation now passing. Silently bless them all. Ask forgiveness, and grant forgiveness. Place the situation in the hands of God, and know that He is there.

Love Is Everywhere

God's love will always find a way to express itself. One of the reasons we grasp at good things is because we think if we don't, we'll be left out of the joy in life. But of course the controlling and needy behavior that results from such a belief is sure to keep our good at bay. It's when we settle into the depths of who we are, knowing that's enough, and let other people be whoever they need to be and go wherever they need to go that the universe delivers our optimal good in a way we can receive it.

Love is everywhere, but if our eyes aren't open to see it, we miss out. Who among us hasn't missed out on love because we were looking for it in one package and it came in another? Our problem is rarely a lack of love so much as a mental block to our awareness of its presence.*

Once I was speaking to a teenager about her problems with her friends at school. She was sad because a group of girls who had been so close the year before were no longer so, and Hayley felt left out of the new group. She felt rejected and bereft, thinking she no longer had good friends.

"Hey, Hayley!" I said. "You've got to diversify!"

"What do you mean?" she asked, looking at me through adorable, tear-filled eyes.

"I mean love is everywhere! I mean there are other relationships to experience—not just those! It means you're more tied to those particular kids being the source of love in your life than you need to be. People are free, and you want to let them go when they're not moved to be close to you. But that doesn't lessen the amount of love that's available to you. Release them, bless them, feel your loss, and release it to God. I promise you—there's a miracle up ahead."

We said a prayer in which we surrendered to God her relationship with those girlfriends and asked that her heart be opened to receive the love that God intended for her. A couple of months later I saw Hayley as she ran into her house, chatting away, obviously happy. She was talking with her mother about going to a movie with a couple of friends. I asked if there had been some changes on the friendship front.

"Well, kinda!" she said. "But mainly, I have these new friends! It's fantastic!" I spoke with her for a moment about how the first situation, an apparent loss, led to something good. She had learned to release what was apparently no longer hers so that something new and wonderful could make its way into her life.

She agreed and then said to me, "I think I had a miracle."

I know she did.

Relationships That Mend the Heart

The Holy Spirit has many ways of paving a path for us, saving us from the pain of our own delusions. Sometimes it's a teacher or a book. And often it's simply another human being.

I'm often grateful for how much help I receive from people around me who can see something I can't see at a time when I most need to see it. Someone will just happen to call, and I'll just happen to tell them what's going on, and they'll just happen to share their thoughts in a way that brings the clarity my mind was seeking or the peace my soul was longing for.

The closer we grow to God, the closer we grow to our natural talent at protecting our brothers.* The more aligned we are with the love of God, the better we are at being true friends. We know how to be there, to say the right things, to give casual counsel to the people we love.

There are three people I often talk to on the telephone late at night. If someone were to ask me to write down on a piece of paper my most significant activities, I probably wouldn't write, "Talking to Richard, Victoria, and Suzannah and telling them everything." Yet it *is* one of my most important activities because it clears my head for everything else. In fact, I think such phone calls are more important than they appear.

Sociologists have now amended a traditional theory about how people respond to stress. As it turns out, the "fight or flight" syndrome that had been taken as gospel for the last few decades was derived from research based on the reactions of men only. When women were added to the research, researchers found another kind of reaction: "tend or mend." In other words, women tend to build relationships as our primary response to stress.

All of us have male and female aspects to our psyche; all of us fight or flee sometimes, and all of us tend or mend sometimes. But when we call each other to process our thoughts and feelings, it's no accident that those calls often happen late at night, when a deeper quiet is available to the soul. From the earliest days of recorded history, people told stories around nighttime campfires. We share stories as a way of holding our psyches, indeed our cultures, together. It is difficult to feel the love of God when the love of others is unavailable. The times when we bring His comfort to each other is hardly a less important time of day.

Where We Are Now

We are at a place where few of us can move forward without the help of another. Not because we are not whole but finally—at last—because we are. We are no longer fractions of ourselves looking for others to complete us. We are fairly whole—and now what?

Now we must conceive new life from deep inside ourselves. For that to occur, we must be in relationship. To cocreate life, we need each other—and God's help.

The miracle of love draws us to each other. And into that union God pours forth Himself. We will become, in each other's arms and in His as well, a new humanity. We will conceive something new. We will grow wings of divine compassion and intelligence, and the entire world will change. God Himself will rejoice.

And life will go on.

CHAPTER NINE

From *Spiritual Death* to *Rebirth*

Wh
hen I was in junior high school, I really liked chemistry. On the other hand, I was a terrible chemistry student. My teacher had no place in her thinking for someone who was a terrible student but really liked chemistry anyway. In her mind, there was either "good chemistry student" or "bad chemistry student." And she let me know which one I was.

Pow! Any belief in myself as a science student died right there.

Perhaps a parent told you that you would never be pretty, and any belief in your beauty died right there. Perhaps someone told you that you were dumb and would never amount to anything, and your self-confidence died right there. Or someone told you that you had no talent and would never be able to play in an orchestra, and your belief in your musical ability died right there.

For most of us, there's not a tomb big enough to hold the bones of the parts of ourselves that died along the way.

The you that has been invalidated, put down, suppressed, violated, hurt, endangered, smeared, humiliated, mocked, brutalized, abandoned, lied about, stolen from—on and on goes the list of ego delight—such is your crucified self.

The crucifixion is not specifically a Christian concept; metaphysically, it is a pattern of energy, demonstrated physically in the life of Jesus but experienced psychically in the life of everyone. Energetically, it symbolizes a pattern of thought. Death is its mission and life its enemy, for it is the mind at work against God.

Thus the drama of every human life, as love is born into the world and then crucified by fear. But the story does not stop there. Resurrection, like crucifixion, is a metaphysical truth: it is God's response to the ego, or the ultimate triumph of love. All that is ever going on, in any situation, is that love appears, it is crucified, and ultimately love holds sway.

One night I was watching *Dances with Wolves* on television with my daughter. Both of us were deeply moved by the lives of the Sioux Indians—their harmony with nature and spirit, the way they allowed the ways of true, essential being to order their lives and bless their world. They treated life itself as a sacred treasure. Yet the collective ego of the Western world tried to destroy, and ultimately succeeded in destroying, their civilization of that time.

Such are the tragedies of human history. There *is* a dark force, not outside us but within us, always at work to destroy the love that God creates. That force, or ego, is held in place by our belief that we are separate from God and from each other; it expresses itself constantly through judgment and blame. It is every unkind word, attack, thought, or violent action. Sometimes it whispers, as in a mean glance; sometimes it shouts, as in the genocide of a people. But it is always active, as long as it has fear to fuel it. And today it has its eye on the biggest prize of all—the prospect of global annihilation.

Sometimes it's other people who string us up on the cross, and at other times we do it all by ourselves. Frequently, it seems to be a combination of both. The ego does not discriminate so much as it seeks to harm whoever it can reach. But the part of us that can be crucified is not the part of us that is who we actually are. The ego can destroy the body, but it cannot destroy the spirit.

Crucifixion takes many forms: material, mental, emotional, and spiritual. Mentally, it is a progressive disease at work within all our minds. It is sometimes called the second force, the anti-Christ, the devil. It is the destructive, anti-life element in the human experience.

All forms of ego have ultimate destruction as their goal. Alcoholism and drug addiction don't want to merely inconvenience you; they want to kill you. A terminal disease doesn't want to inconvenience you; it wants to kill you. Escalating violence doesn't want to inconvenience you; it wants to kill you. God knows this, and He has answered: He has sent His holiness to save us from ourselves. And as we embrace our holiness and the changes it engenders within us, He has a plan for what comes next.

The resurrection is God's answer to the crucifixion; it is His uplifting of our consciousness to the point where the effects of fear are canceled. Our holiness—God's love within us—is the only way humankind has ever transcended darkness, and it is the only way we ever will.

"Jesus wept," as we all do, challenged in our various ways by the lies and projections of the ego. Jesus's crucifixion—the torture and murder of an innocent man—is a radical teaching example, a demonstration of the strength of fear and then the power of love to overcome it. Jesus died, then lay in his tomb for three days. And for that period of time, of course, it seemed to those who loved him as if all hope were lost. Yet hope is of God, and what is of God is never lost.

Jesus transcended the crucifixion by taking it on, as it were. Confronted with the murderous projections of others, he continued to love with an open heart. And by allowing his heart to be as big as the universe, he became a vortex of the miraculous. Just as in the presence of Moses the laws of time and space were suspended in the parting of the Red Sea, in the presence of Jesus, the laws of death were suspended as well.

What did Jesus have that we don't have? Nothing. The issue is not that he had something we don't have, but that he didn't have anything else.* His love of God had cast out all else, leaving only the eternally true.

Collective Darkness

Today our personal crucifixions are particularly intense, as we take on the individual pieces of a huge and cosmic darkness. It's a universal pattern that the darkness seeks to destroy the light, and no one ever said, "Except in your case." And the darkness is most intense when it senses encroachment by the light. If you're doing good things and extending loving energies, then the second force is on its way to you. But that doesn't mean it's *about* you.

In today's world, to truly make a stand for holiness, for universal love, is in most situations so far from the status quo that you have to decide how much you're willing to compromise your heart in order to get along. The world as we know it is dominated by fear, and some of our major institutions are its unwitting headquarters. Think this way, don't think that way. Go in this direction, not in that one. Yet the spirit isn't known for conformity. Where there is no room for the ecstatic impulse, there is no real room for the revelation of love.

If you can rise above the fear in your life and live the love within you, and if I can rise above my fear and live the love in me—if that drama is reenacted enough times by enough of the world's people—then we will pierce the cosmic darkness and tip the world in the direction of light. Every one of us counts, and there is no such thing as a neutral thought.* Every perception leads to more fear or more love, for us and the world around us. With every prayer, every act of kindness, and every thought of forgiveness, we are building a wave of love that will turn back fear.

But we cannot take on the fear of the world until first we have taken it on within ourselves. And that we cannot do alone. We can't heal ourselves of a deep neurosis simply by intellectually deciding to change. Many of us have tried and failed.

God can do for us, however, what we cannot do for ourselves. When His spirit comes upon us, fear is silenced. It is nullified. It is gone. Once we have embraced the fullness of our spirit, then the effects of our former brokenness disappear. From physical disorders to painful relationships, from world hunger to world conflict, once we have risen to our divine potential, we will become people with the courage and intelligence to cast out darkness. With God in charge, we will rise above the thoughts that keep us bound. And thus the world will be changed. We can forego a collective Armageddon if we learn the lessons from our personal ones.

Tomb Time

There is metaphysical meaning to the three days between the crucifixion and the resurrection. It symbolizes the time it takes for the physical world to catch up with a change in consciousness, for light to ascend again after darkness has overwhelmed us. Resurrection occurs when we hold to love despite appearances and thus invoke a miracle.

Sometimes when we have been deeply wounded, there's a time during which we have to let our souls bleed, take the pain, and wait till the cycle completes itself. You can't rush a river or a heartbreak. Just know that "this too shall pass."

The three days is referred to by a friend of mine as "tomb time," during which it might seem that all hope is lost, when in fact the miracle is just around the corner. Every night is followed by a new day. The ego has its way with us in cruel and vicious ways, to be sure, yet we are delivered by God each day to a new morning—the "promised land" of inner peace.

We have all known crucifixion and then lived through a tomb time when it seemed as though the light in our lives might never return. Yet the movement of the universe is always in the direction of ultimate love; in the words of Martin Luther King Jr., "The arc of the moral universe is long, but it bends toward justice." The ego roars, but God will always have the final say.

Our crucifixions deal us a material blow, but in the hands of God the blow can become a spiritual gift. No matter what occurs in our lives, we can become better people because of it. If we had not stumbled, we could not have gotten back up. And now that we have gotten up, our backbones are a little straighter and our heads a little higher. There is nothing more beautiful than the mantle of survivor. There is nothing more illuminated than the resurrected body, the new personality that emerges when the old one has been laid to rest.

In the words of Charles Swindoll, a pastor and radio Bible teacher in the mid-twentieth century, "I have tried and I cannot find, either in scripture or history, a strong-willed individual whom God used greatly until He allowed them to be hurt deeply."

I remember once watching Richard Nixon in a television interview years after he had left the White House. He spoke with a wisdom and compassion I had never seen him exhibit during his time in politics. A president for whom I had previously felt such disdain had become a different person. And how could he have not? Given the crucifixion he endured—brought entirely upon himself—how could he have done other than to have either died or broken through to another place? Clearly, he had done the latter. A failure that in worldly terms is almost impossible to fathom had led to a spiritual success.

Crucifixions take us into the darkness of the soul, where we wrestle with the demons of shame and loathing, anger and hatred. We are asked to die to so many parts of ourselves—to lay down both sword and shield, to give up judgment and willfulness and hate. Yet when we stand there naked, having forgiven so much, we can feel a sense of lightness return to our hearts, and we know we have made it to another place. Crucifixion is never the end; in a way, it is just the beginning.

With every scar, we become carriers of the universal wound as well as transmitters of a universal healing. When we have suffered and transcended our suffering, we emerge with sacred knowledge embedded in our cells. In our life at least, some darkness has been overcome. And we will be led to others who have similarly overcome, as well as to those who have not yet but will be inspired to in our presence. Together, we will form a unified field of resurrective possibility, an opening that does not just bless our own lives but the entire world. And that is what is occurring on the planet today. People are feeling the pain of the world, almost like an inoculation. We are hurrying to rise up so we can create a higher field for everyone.

The women around Jesus waited and prayed at his feet while he was crucified. These women symbolize the friends who bear witness to our crucifixions and care about our suffering. When they go to the tomb to claim the body—that is, when they have empathized with our pain and now accompany us on our psychic journey back to wholeness—they often find that the person we were before no longer exists.

They find, when the spirit of God has moved in us, that we were not defeated but rather we became our better selves. We died to who we used to be, that's true, but who we will be now is a spirit reborn and refreshed. The fever has broken, the tears have dried, and we emerge again into the light of our true being. Such is the resurrection, the light of God upon our souls.

Rebirth

There is passion to the crucifixion, but there is passion to the resurrection as well. It cannot be seen with physical eyes, however, for the emergence of a reborn self is not a material occurrence. You have the same eyes, but there is a new light in them. You have the same brain, but it operates differently. You have the same heart, but it is beating with His now. And the resurrection is not a moment but a pattern. For every two steps into the light, we might fall one step back into darkness. But once we are on the way up, once we have glimpsed the One who has promised to take us there, there is no real going back.

It doesn't matter what anyone says or does to try to stop you. You're on your way to a brand-new life, not just for yourself but for others as well. You are not a martyr; you're a teacher of love. You have seen the light, and you are walking toward it.

Just know who you are and Who lives within you. He is risen, and so are you.

The Power of Faith

In both the Bible and *A Course in Miracles* it is stated, "Blessed are those who have faith who cannot see." It's easy to believe in love when you're surrounded by kindness; it's not so easy when you're confronted with the judgments and the attacks of the world.

Faith is an aspect of consciousness. We either have faith in the love that is eternally true or faith in the illusions of the ego. In that sense, there is no such thing as a faithless person. If you have faith in the reality of disaster, then disaster will be real for you. If you have faith in a reality of love that lies beyond a disaster, then you become an opening for its transformation. The miracle worker does not look *away* from darkness, but *through* it to the light beyond. Faith is a kind of positive denial: we don't deny that something is happening in the physical world. We simply have faith that this reality is but mere illusion before the love of God. We deny the ultimate reality of the world itself.

Does your faith lie in the reality of the crucifixion or in the reality of the resurrection?

We tend to have greater faith in the limitations of the world than in the limitlessness of God's power. When the disciples of Jesus thought they were going to drown, their faith lay in the power of the storm. When Jesus came out and walked on water, He didn't say to His disciples, "O ye of little walking-on-water proficiency; didn't you read the brochure?" He said, "O ye of little faith."

Faith means we're open to the possibility of miracles, knowing that when we stand on the ground of love, within the space of holiness, then all material forces are automatically programmed to work on our behalf. We don't have to *do* anything new so much as *become* someone new in order to fundamentally change our lives. And then we do not just believe in the resurrection; we *share* the resurrection. As we humble ourselves and step back with our ego, allowing God to lead the way, miracles occur naturally. No stress, no strain.

A Change of Heart

While traveling in Amsterdam several months ago, I noticed that something about myself had changed. I have traveled extensively since I was a child and visited scores of museums throughout the world. I have always delighted in portraits, landscapes, sculpture, Oriental screens, decorative arts, jewelry design, and all the other visual treats that are offered in such places. But one particular category of painting never moved me, and I always passed it by without giving much attention. That was nautical art: ships in the harbor, ships on the sea, ships wherever. It simply wasn't my thing.

But if you're visiting museums in Holland, you're going to see pictures of boats. And this time, for whatever reason, they touched me in a different way. This time, when I saw a painting of a ship on a rough sea, facing the clear possibility of shipwreck, my mind went to the sailors who were on the ship, the reasons they were there, the terror they were feeling, and whether or not they survived. I thought about their loved ones on land and what they felt when they heard there was a storm at sea. I thought about whether the painter had ever seen such a roiling ocean, and if he hadn't, how did he know what it looked like? I realized that for many years I had looked at those paintings, yet I hadn't really seen them at all. For I had brought nothing of my heart to the experience.

On the same trip, I visited the house of Anne Frank. It's been years since I read *The Diary of Anne Frank*, and I thought I had internalized her story and its meaning. Yet visiting the Anne Frank museum with my daughter on this trip, I could barely stop crying—in fact, I couldn't stop crying—as I walked through the rooms of her family's house. Seeing where she slept, unable to run outside and play or even look at sunlight through the window; seeing the places on her wall where her father pasted pictures from magazines so it wouldn't seem quite so dreary; thinking of the extraordinary, daily tension and fear that were experienced by those hiding in those rooms as well as by their friends who were hiding them; thinking of all the years they survived that way, only to have their hiding place betrayed a year before the end of the war; and thinking of Anne's horrifying days at Bergen-Belsen concentration camp, only to die one month before the liberation of the camps—I could hardly bear the weight of such sorrow, mixed with Anne's profound and compassionate insights into the nature of the human heart. I thought about her father's survival, his learning of his family's death, his publishing Anne's diaries—and always with the realization that this same tale of suffering was experienced not once but six million times.

As we walked through the rooms and read the exhibits, I told my daughter how important it is to bear witness to the suffering of others. For such pain as the Frank family's is experienced still, all over the world, by people as unfortunate today as they were then. And only if we allow ourselves to grieve for them all will we devote ourselves, as God would have us do, to creating a different kind of world.

At one point my daughter said to me sweetly, "Oh, Mommy, please don't cry." And I thought to myself, "Oh, Emma, please do."

There are those who would not visit such a museum, who would rather shut themselves off and not feel the agony or face the horror of all the suffering in the world. We do whatever we can to distance ourselves from it. But when Jesus said to the disciples who were falling asleep in the Garden of Gethsemane, "What, can you not remain awake with me one hour?" I think he was referring to our need to remain awake when others suffer. If nothing else, doing so reminds us how extraordinarily fortunate we are—and I do mean extraordinarily fortunate—to have a roof over our heads, food in our stomachs, and the right to simply see sunlight each day. As long as that is not true for everyone, there is much, much work for us to do on this earth. And if we will not do it, who will?

Even when there is nothing we can specifically do to help those who suffer, remaining awake to their predicament exudes its own kind of moral force. There are those in the world—imprisoned, in pain—for whom the difference between choosing life and choosing death lies simply in knowing that someone cares.

After visiting the Anne Frank house, I sat drinking coffee at a café right across the canal. On the same street where she so longed to run and play but could not, I was free to wander and shop and sip coffee and laugh out loud. By what gift of fate am I so fortunate?

There is a building in Amsterdam where all Jews were rounded up by the Nazis for deportation to the concentration camps, where many of them would be gassed immediately upon arrival. A plaque on the building says we should take a moment and remember them. In that moment, I think the departed souls feel our blessing; hopefully, in some way, it helps bring them peace.

As for us, may it bring us depth. May our hearts explode from the sheer size of it all. For therein lies the only real hope for humankind.

Resurrection

It is the consciousness of peace, not the behavior of war, that will ultimately turn back the tides of fear. And it is incumbent upon each of us to foster that consciousness. I am not referring to just making things better; I am referring to transcending all physical laws, bending the rules of time and space, and coming alive where we were previously dead. It's time to see miracles in our own lives, to be resurrected from the littleness of our former selves. Through God, these things are possible. These miracles are available, and they are necessary now.

It doesn't matter what someone said when you were a child; you know now that you're smart and attractive. It doesn't matter what happened before; you can rise up now and start over. It doesn't matter what they did to you; forgiveness has washed you clean.

Boys who have become men will now become great men; girls who have become women will now become great women. We will give birth to our better selves. Those who rise to the heights of their potential will not be the exception; they will be the rule. Through them—and by *them*, I mean *us*—a plan will emerge for the salvation of the world.

A new world awaits all of us, as our minds are healed by love.

CHAPTER TEN

From *Your Plan*
to *God's Plan*

*A*n underground revolution is sweeping the hearts
and minds of the people of the world, and it is
happening despite the wars and terror that confront us. This revolution is a fundamental change of worldview, and it carries with
it the potential to reorganize the structure of human civilization.
It brings a basic shift in the thoughts that dominate the world. It
wages a peace that will end all war. It is a global phenomenon
that will change the cellular structure of the human race. To
those who are part of it, who feel called to it, its reality is a
growing if not obvious truth. To still others, it's a lofty but
ridiculous notion, a preposterous and silly idea.

Yet no social revolution of any import emerged because
everybody woke up one day saying, "I get it! I get it!" Such revo-
lutions emerged instead from what anthropologist Margaret
Mead described as "a small group of concerned citizens." Not
only are such groups capable of changing the world, according to
Mead, but in fact, they're the only thing that ever has. And they
are doing it now.

A spiritually attuned counterculture is already in our midst. It is marked not by clothes or music, drugs or sex, as was the counterculture of the sixties, but by the internal attitudes of those who perceive it. They make suggestions and comments that are just a little bit wiser; they bring new insights into areas previously locked down by the status quo. They see some star in the sky that not everyone is seeing. And in their presence, we start to see it too.

Signing Up for Duty

We sign up for duty, for participation in this revolution, through a sincere desire to be used by something larger than ourselves, for the purpose of healing the world. It doesn't even matter if we don't call that "something larger" by the name of God. For some people conspire with God who do not yet believe in Him.* It is ultimately not our belief but our experience that matters.* God has no ego by which to be insulted if we do not get His name right.

But whatever name we call Him, we come to realize that we are the army, but He is in charge. He cannot use us to change the world deeply until first we have been changed by Him. To surrender the world to Him, first we must surrender ourselves.

The change begins with a shift in the lens through which we perceive the world. It grows within us to affect not only our own lives, but also the lives of those around us. It leads us to connect with others who are similarly undergoing a transformation of their ego structures, from an old perspective to something new. And through our individual and collective efforts, divinely inspired, we will turn the world around in time. Just when we thought all hope was ended, hope will reappear.

For those of us who are cynical; for those of us who are too tired now; for those of us who are weary of the way things always go; for those of us who used to care but are too busy now just trying to get by, there is a change afoot. It begins in the heart. And as it rises to the surface, it will change all things.

IMAGINE THAT GOD HAS ASKED YOU if He could use your hands and feet, to go where He would have you go and do what He would have you do.

Imagine that God has asked you if He could use your mouth, to say what He would have you say and to whom.

Imagine these things because He has.

"Many are called, but few are chosen" means that everyone is called but few care to listen.* The call goes out to all of us, all the time. None of us has more or less capacity for contributing to the salvation of the world.

Choosing to serve God, we are choosing the path toward God's greatness within us. When we see people who are clearly letting the spirit work through them—who have found their genius, their power, their passion—we are not seeing some special force at work that chose them over others. The power did not choose them so much as they chose *it*.

Those among us who have achieved the most have achieved only a fraction of what all of us are capable of.* The "gifts of the Holy Spirit" are waiting for all of us, when our lives are dedicated to God's plan.

Every morning, we have a choice: Will I seek out God's plan today, or will I go about my day as a slave to my ego's agenda? To choose God's plan is to choose the option with the best opportunity for turning your life into a conduit for the miraculous. As soon as we start asking Him how we can help with His plan, rather than just asking Him to help with *our* plans, everything will be better for everyone.

We're here to be teachers of God—that is, those who demonstrate love. God has a plan for the salvation of the world, called "the plan for the teachers of God."* His teachers come from all religions and no religion.* There is nothing to sign up for, no worldly organization or institution to belong to. It simply refers to a stirring in the heart, which then activates an internal guidance system already present within us. If we *ask* how to help, He will show us how to help.

While there are hate-filled people planning ways to sow violence and destruction on earth, God has a blueprint for creating peace on earth. It's not a physical blueprint, but rather a plan that exists in His Mind, pieces of it ready to be downloaded into the mind of anyone who asks to receive his or her part. Each of us carries maximal potential to be used by God to heal the world.

He has a plan. And it cannot not work.

Our Father's Business

Sometimes, going about "our Father's business" involves something we *don't* do as much as something we do. It can be our passive resistance, even more than a direct challenge, that subverts an unjust influence.

I knew a minister whose job was terminated unjustly, and the board of directors at his church chose to assassinate his character to avoid any challenge from his congregation. He was understandably upset, yet the actions of many friends who supported him touched his heart.

One was a woman who cut his hair every month. After the minister's dismissal from the church, one of the board members, a man who had been largely responsible for the campaign against him, began going to her to have his hair cut as well. Every month the man would come in, sit in her salon chair, and repeat the same mischaracterization of the facts, steeped in self-serving untruths and denial.

After a couple of months, the woman simply didn't wish to cut the board member's hair anymore. She no longer felt good about doing business with him. Her loyalty to her friend, and standing firm in a principle of righteousness as she understood it, mattered more to her than business. She couldn't understand, she said, how a place could abuse people and still call itself a church. She called the board member to say she no longer wished to cut his hair.

The woman's action was a demonstration of Mahatma Gandhi's principle of nonviolence, which declares that *moral force emanates from righteous action*. While such force might not have observable effects, it indeed has effects on an invisible plane. By simply standing in Truth—not only in our words but through our behavior as well—we help create a wave of power that will heal the world.

In 1955 Rosa Parks sparked the civil rights movement by simply saying no to the white bus driver who told her to give up her seat for a white man. When Dr. Martin Luther King Jr. called for a boycott of the Montgomery bus company, he was calling for a huge sacrifice on the part of hundreds of people. For 381 days, people walked miles to work, sometimes enduring terrorism and harassment, rather than continue to participate in a system of segregated busing. By simply saying no to what she knew to be unjust, Mrs. Parks demonstrated the tremendous powers such action sets in motion.

We never know what effect our simply standing on truth might have. We think, "I'm just one person; what difference can I make?" But none of us is "just one person." All minds are joined, and each of us has a chance every day to say yes to something that could make the world a better place and no to something that degrades it. We're sometimes looking for the big plan that will save the world, while not recognizing our own part in it. The plan that will save us involves little ways that each of us becomes more righteous every day. And enough tiny droplets, in time, make up an ocean.

The woman who refused to cut the hair of someone she knew had wronged her friend did not just help her friend. She helped herself as well. By fueling the forces of loyalty and integrity, she generated moral power that added to her own spiritual stature.

No action goes unregistered by the universe. The political philosopher Edmund Burke wrote, "The only thing necessary for evil to triumph is for enough good people to do nothing." And the only thing that will triumph over evil is for enough good people to actually *do good*.

It's not enough to simply talk about goodness. The fact that I say I love you means little unless it's acted on. The fact that I say I love you means little unless you experience me as a loyal and ethical friend. The fact that I say I love you does not make everything all right if my behavior argues otherwise. That is often the problem with a so-called spiritual worldview: there are those who act as though the use of the *L* word renders an authentic effort at ethics, integrity, loyalty, or even honesty unnecessary. But surely God is less impressed by our words than by our deeds.

In the movie *Meet Joe Black*, there is a scene where Death tells a woman's father that he plans to take her with him when he leaves the earth, as he has fallen in love with her and doesn't want to be without her. At that point, her father argues that real love is more than just appetite or even need: it's an active caring for the ultimate well-being of another human being.

Love isn't always easy; and if it doesn't stretch you personally, then it probably isn't love.

The Goal of God's Will

For many of us, the problem is not that we don't believe in God or don't want to be conduits of His love. The problem is simply that we have quite a few other goals as well.* We don't recognize how our separate, individual goals can actually get in the way of God's.

The miracle worker is asked to do two things: see forgiveness as our function, and relinquish all other goals we have invented for ourselves.

Sometimes people ask me about my early years lecturing on *A Course in Miracles* and the interesting ride I've had professionally. Twenty years have passed since I gave my first talk, and from this vantage point I can see clearly why my early accomplishments came effortlessly: I had very little and wanted little more. I was delighted with my apartment, my work, my friends, my life. I was so completely naive to concepts like best-seller status, royalty statements, lecture dates, house payments, public perception, and everything else in the material world that I gave total energy to the work I felt moved to do. My naïveté was an asset.

Walking through a fancy store never used to cause me stress. I couldn't buy anything, and I knew it, so it was like walking through a museum. It's when you can buy one good dress but no more—*that's* when the stress kicks in!

Now, when I read that as a miracle worker I'm supposed to relinquish *any goals I have invented for myself,* I am definitely stopped short. Lecture dates, nest egg, enough for Emma, book contracts—and the list goes on. The world has both rewarded me and imprisoned me. Like many of us, I built a prison around myself and now have the audacity to complain.

So we get caught in a loop: we're trying to escape the pain of a world that *is* the pain. The innocence of ignorance—when we were pure of heart because we simply didn't know anything else—surely must be beautiful to God. But there is another kind of innocence as well: an innocence lost and then regained, having been consciously chosen by one who *does* know something else. It's one thing not to covet because we wouldn't even know what there is to covet, and another thing not to covet because we've been there, done that, and it didn't fix us anyway. Think how useful we are to God then, when our goals have been superseded by His.

Often we try to get clear about what our goals are, figuring out a five- or ten-year plan, making treasure maps, identifying those we wish to emulate. But we should think about our spiritual goals as well. The question shouldn't just be, "Where do I want to be in five or ten years?" It should also be, "*Who* do I want to be in five or ten years?" How long until I move beyond judgment and blame? How long until I stop playing victim? How long until I forgive myself and make the most of the life I have?

Our goal in any situation should be that God's will be done.*

We will be told exactly what we need to know in every instant that our hearts are open.* God speaks to us through what is called "the small still voice for God." Through forgiveness, prayer, and meditation, we can quiet the mind enough to be able to hear it.

One of my favorite prayers in *A Course in Miracles* is the following:

> *Where would you have me go?*
> *What would you have me do?*
> *What would you have me say, and to whom?**

With that prayer, we are asking God to use us—to use our hands and feet and thoughts and feelings. And once we have surrendered ourselves to be used for a higher purpose, we give up the obsession with planning that dominates so much of Western civilization. We know we can't know what's on the other side of a particular turn in the road. We choose to walk across the Holy Spirit's bridge of perception instead, knowing that the destination is not as important as who we are while we are walking.

Inner peace brings more positive experiences into our lives because it aligns us with superior aspects of our own personality. We shift from grandiosity to grandeur and from littleness to magnitude.* We attract rather than repel affection and trust, and—just as important—we develop the power to retain them. It does little good to attract our good if we are too frantic or uncentered to hold onto it once it gets here.

Our Spiritual Magnitude

What will happen as we grow into our spiritual magnitude? In each of our lives, it will look different. Every moment holds infinite possibilities, and how much magnificence we allow to move into us and through us is determined by our willingness and receptivity. To whatever extent the blocks are removed to the awareness of our divine nature, to that extent we are magnetized to the events and situations—and they are magnetized to us—that resonate with our grandeur. If we're vibrating at a low energy, we'll attract low-energy situations (how many times have we stubbed a toe or banged a finger when we were angry?); if we're vibrating at a high energy, we'll attract miracles.

People will call out of nowhere; situations will just seem to improve; abundance of all kinds will just appear. And when they do, it is good to acknowledge them. We often build an altar to our disasters, giving them so much time and attention and energy. But do we do the same for our blessings? Are our minds truly disciplined to call forth and accept the good?

We're living during a "celestial speed-up" in which everything is moving more quickly—including us!* Our issues aren't coming through in slow gentle breezes anymore, but in huge torrential storms! And that's not because we're failing; it's because we're available, God knows it, and *this is it*. I remember watching television one night about the D-Day invasion, how the Allied forces had rehearsed it for months, and then one morning things were different: *this was real.*

This is a critical time in all our lives because it's a critical time on earth. Each of us has the opportunity now to grow into the fullness of our divine potential in order to take our place in God's plan. The plan exists in the Mind of God, and to the extent to which we surrender our thinking to Him, we take our part. Our primary function is to stand in the light of who we are and become the people we are capable of being. From that, all good will follow.

And we step into that light in any moment we choose. When our hearts are closed to love—when we're judgmental, withholding, unforgiving—we are literally *not being ourselves*. We are, in those moments, choosing to be hostage to the ego rather than host to God.

Our function, our happiness, and our purpose all emanate from the same point of power: our capacity to embody love in any given instant. And love is more than "being nice." It is the surrender of a separate sense of self, a claim to the totality of life as part of ourselves. Knowing that we are part of the whole, we shift our perspective from a sense of individual identity to a sense of universal connection. It becomes impossible to act only for yourself when you know that your self includes everyone.

If someone suffers on the other side of the world, he or she is no less a part of ourselves.

And when a critical mass of humanity realizes this, then obstacles to world peace will fade. In the realm of spirit, we see our goal fully accomplished: we want a world remade in the image of love. In the realm of the body, we achieve it gradually: we will do what we can to make the world a better place. Yet the power of the vision keeps the process on track. We know that through our individual efforts, we are contributing to a larger one. Our goal is not just to create a world in which loveless things are outlawed: our vision is a world in which such things have become literally *unthinkable*. That is the role of the miracle worker: to think with so much love that fear begins to lose the false authority by which it rules the world. *Think* of a world in which there is only love, and hold that thought for several minutes each day. The day will come when our thinking will lead to our believing, which will lead to our acting to make it so.

Are We Really Trying?

Everyone I know wants the world to change. All of us want to be part of the solution. We find the thought of the complete revolution of human values a very attractive idea. Everyone's all ready to sign up. Let's go!

But wait. You start to hear a few little complaints. "Can we do this when *The West Wing* isn't on?" "Could I sign up for a slot between two and four on Saturday, when the kids are at soccer?" "Couldn't we meet in a nicer place?" We're the only generation in the history of the world that wants to reinvent society over white wine and brie.

Only in America would someone expect changing the world to be *convenient!* Hello. Reality check: The suffragettes had no cell phones. The abolitionists had no faxes.

They did have love in their hearts, however. And so do you and I.

I asked a friend what I should speak about at a talk I was to give in his bookshop, and he said, "Speak about the challenges of living a spiritual life today—I mean, we all try so hard!"

And I thought to myself, "No, we don't!"

For whatever reason, however, we keep telling ourselves we do. We're all revisionists these days, and we're not content to just revise our past—we even revise the present. We seem to have a magical belief that if we describe ourselves a certain way, then it must be true.

We talk about how hard it is to live a spiritual life when we're not even meditating regularly or making the deepest effort to forgive those who have hurt us. Perhaps we have spent so many years in the classroom that "student mode" has become a habit.

It's time to graduate. Enough of us know spiritual principles now; we've read the same books and listened to the same tapes. It's time to *become* the principles now, to embody them and demonstrate them in our daily lives. Until we do, we will not really learn them at the deepest level. They will not inform our souls or transform the world.

And if that's the case, we will go down in history as the generation that knew what we needed to know yet didn't do what we needed to do. I can't imagine how it would feel, to die with that realization.

We've subscribed to a kind of ivory tower notion of spiritual education: keep it abstract and intellectual and safe. Yet the spoils of history usually go to those willing to get dirt underneath their fingernails.

I heard a woman talking recently about her frustration with politics: "We've tried so hard, and nothing ever seems to change!" I thought she must be joking.

"Uh, no, we haven't. How many of us even vote?" I asked her. "And if we do, what does that mean—we go to the voting booth every two or four years? Where do we get off thinking that we've *tried so hard?*" Are we thinking we made some supreme and noble effort to change the world, and it didn't *work?!* We've been so trained by thirty-minute sitcoms that if we don't get what we want in half an hour, it's like, uh-oh, we tried but failed. Too bad. It's over. Next.

Mother Teresa made a supreme and noble effort. Martin Luther King Jr. made a supreme and noble effort. Susan B. Anthony made a supreme and noble effort. We have not made a supreme and noble effort. In fact, most of us make very little effort to change the world. But then we feel frustrated when we see that it's not changing!

Usually, when people say, "We've tried so hard!" they're not really talking about themselves. It's more like, "Well, there are other people I know who have!" It's laughable when you think about it. Perhaps we don't realize the big secret in our midst—which isn't how *little* power we have to change things, but rather how *much* power we have that we aren't using! We're like birds who were never informed, or have forgotten, we have wings.

But a great remembering is reverberating among us, and whatever we've done or haven't done, succeeded at or failed at; whatever time we've used well or time we've wasted; we are here, we are available, we are present to the moment and up to the challenge.

All we need remember is this: if God has given us a job to do, He will provide for us the means by which to accomplish it.* All we have to do is ask Him what He wants us to do and then be willing to do it.

Goals

Before a spiritual awakening, we live our lives pretty much on our own. We go into situations with our worldly thought forms usually centered around our own agenda, our individual goals, and our needs as we define them. Yet once we're on the miracle worker's path, we start to surrender our goals to God.

Sometimes I have found myself being fairly surrendered in deciding what to do, yet grab the controls when it comes to how I go about doing it. It's not enough to allow God to decide what action to take. We have to also allow the Spirit of God to deeply influence who we are within the action.

You might feel guided to a certain meeting. But if your thoughts during the meeting are arrogant or judgmental, if your behavior is controlling or immature, then even if you're where you "should" be, you still blow it once you're there! Our personal energy both attracts and repels our good. People telepathically feel the tenor of our thoughts, and very few people jump up and down to be with a negative person.

If I walk into a room and silently bless everyone in it, no one will know exactly why they feel more peaceful, but they will. When our thoughts are aligned with God's, we are lifted into a greater realm of possibility than our ego-based thinking can provide. It is not enough to pray, "Dear God, should I go to this meeting?" It's also helpful to remember, before walking into it, to pray, "Dear God, now that I'm here, I surrender this meeting to you. May I be an instrument of your peace. Amen."

We often ignore the amazing power of prayer, and for an equally amazing reason: *we don't believe it could be that easy.* Yet is it difficult for the rosebud to blossom? Is it difficult for the stars to shine? Part of God's genius is that He makes it all look so easy. We keep looking for the wings of a sparrow when the wings of an eagle have already been given us.* We keep clinging to our weakness while our true strength is huge.

Trading Ambition for Inspiration

The point is not to do something or not do it. The point is to do something if we're internally guided to do so and not to do something if we're not guided to do so. Sometimes people think they have a great idea, and then it falls apart. Yet if the plan was self-initiated rather than divinely inspired, then it might not have reflected the best use of your talents in a particular area.

Miracle workers are warned to "avoid self-initiated plans."* What this means is that ideas we come up with ourselves—ideas that come not from a sense of deeper guidance and inspiration but rather from a sense of ambition and a desire for control—come from the ego self and are not backed by the heavens. Quite simply, they are not blessed. They might be good ideas, and very well intentioned, but if they do not emanate from the Holy Spirit, then they represent "my will" and not "Your will." Our good intentions are not enough; our willingness is everything.*

Often I've heard people complain about a plan that failed. "But it was a good idea! I don't know why it didn't succeed!" But though we might have thought something was a good idea, the mortal mind has a limited perspective on "good ideas." By what criteria can we discern a truly good idea, given our inability to know what will happen in the future, what lessons need to be learned by whom, and how our actions fit into God's larger plan? A blessed idea does not come from the mortal mind, which has no idea how our talents and abilities would work best within a larger unfolding good. And from a spiritual perspective, there *is* a larger plan of unfolding good, a will-to-healing that is built into the workings of the universe. We will be told everything we need to know and shown everything we need to see. The Whole (Holy) Mind (Spirit) of God impresses itself upon us when we pray and meditate and seek to follow spiritual principles. As we open ourselves to receive His guidance, our thoughts and feelings fall into patterns that lead all things within and around us to realms of divine right order.

Ministry Is Not Just for Ministers

When I was a young woman, I remember being overwhelmed with the thought that I didn't know what I should do with my life. I had no inkling that there might already be a divinely ordained plan, some track I simply had to ride my train along. I thought I was responsible for the train *and* the track. No wonder they were both so poorly built at times.

Following God's way is not so difficult as it is different.* What's difficult is retraining our minds, getting over our resistance to thinking in such a different way than we've been taught. If in fact our only function is love and forgiveness, then the entire world as we know it is wrong. And it is. The thinking of the world is 180 degrees away from the thinking of God.*

It takes a certain humility to present ourselves truly empty and available to God. But when we do, we become filled with information we don't otherwise possess. Like what to do with our lives—which is significant information to be lacking.

We're always wondering whether we should do this or that when from a spiritual perspective what's most important is not what we *do* so much as who we *become*. Some things God indeed would have us do, but first we must become different people in order to know how to or to be able to. God can't work for us until He can work through us.

Once I was taking a vacation and had been working with a travel agent named Connie. At the last minute, because of a work commitment, I needed to change my date of departure. When Connie looked into it, however, she found that she had sold me a completely nonrefundable and unchangeable ticket.

I was upset because I would not have bought the ticket had I known that. But I also knew that this was a great opportunity for me to strike the balance between asserting appropriate displeasure regarding someone's professional performance and showing grace and compassion toward someone who had simply made a mistake. As my fourteen-year-old daughter said to me after listening to my end of the phone call, "You did great, Mom. You let her know she had done it wrong, but you didn't *shame* her."

From a purely mortal perspective, God's plan might have been that I take a vacation. But on a deeper level, God's plan had to do with what Connie and I both learned from that experience: she, to be more careful in the work she was doing for her clients, and I, to handle such a situation without being either too easy or too hard on someone around me.

No matter what greatness might otherwise unfold in Connie's life, it's blocked if she's not performing at her best. And no matter what greatness might unfold in my life, it's blocked by whatever issues I might have in dealing with people. And *that* is God's plan—that the blocks to our inner light be removed, that His light might then shine through.

The *Course in Miracles* workbook exercise "I am among the ministers of God" says, "It is not our part to judge our worth, nor can we know what role is best for us; what we can do within a larger plan we cannot see in its entirety. . . ." It continues,

Whatever your appointed role may be, it was selected by the Voice for God, Whose function is to speak for you as well. Seeing your strengths exactly as they are, and equally aware of where they can be best applied, for what, to whom and when, He chooses and accepts your part for you. He does not work without your own consent.

. . . You become aware at last there is one Voice in you.

And that one Voice appoints your function, and relays it to you, giving you the strength to understand it, do what it entails, and succeed in everything you do that is related to it.

Sometimes someone says, "Well, I'd love to be off doing God's work, but I've got three kids at home—I can't go anywhere!" Yet ministry is determined by its content, not its form. There is certainly no ministry more important than parenting. Being conscious and attentive in your dealings with a fifteen-year-old trying to figure out how to get through high school is as important as feeding AIDS patients in Africa. If more people running the world today had been raised with greater spiritual awareness when they were fifteen years old, perhaps the world wouldn't be in the mess it's in now.

The Holy Spirit assigns each of us to the place our talents and abilities can best be put to use and our lessons most powerfully learned.* Don't doubt the plan; just make yourself available to it.

A while ago, I was visiting my mother, talking to her and her nurse. Years ago I would have been impatient, thinking I needed to be out in the world trying to do something important. What I know now is that the world is wherever I am, and my lessons for both teaching and learning are right here, right now, in this case with my mom and her nurse. For I might have things to teach them, but even more importantly, they most certainly have things to teach me. Like getting over myself. Like being more patient. Like showing gratitude to the woman who gave me my life. Just little things like that, ha ha . . .

MY HOUSEMATE (the one with the motorcycles, who rarely checks his messages) once called from a vacation and told me he had met a woman he liked very much, and he was bringing her home for a visit. I was happy he had met someone, but I felt some fear regarding our living arrangement. Was she going to live in the house with us? Would she like my daughter, and would she like me? Would I still feel comfortable in my home? What if she didn't like us and wanted us to move out?

I allowed my monkey mind to do what it needed to do, yet I remembered that my only mission is to love. For hours before I met her, I simply prayed that our meeting would be blessed. I asked to be an instrument of love in her life. I asked that my heart be opened to her, that our relationship reach its highest possibility. I knew that if I put my heart and mind in the right place, the future would reach its highest expression. I am not here to design God's universe but to allow Him to show me the design He has already created. It was created in total love, for me and all living things. My mission is to trust that.

Love is infinite, and infinitely creative. If that woman is coming into the house, then that is my blessing for the day. It is part of my spiritual curriculum. It's what's up, and that's how I know it's important. Reality now is the reality that matters. Whatever is happening is our opportunity to heal our wounded parts, should our hearts and minds be open to God's love.

It was going to be a lesson no matter what: either a lesson in being open to a new situation or a lesson in setting boundaries with compassion. But the key to learning the lesson lay in opening my heart. Only in that way was I doing my part to move the universe and myself toward divine right order.

Running my mind along that track, I prepared the way for higher things to unfold. And they did. We were friends by the end of the evening.

God Is Not Your Gofer

Sometimes we talk to God as though we're giving Him our shopping list. *Please do this for me, and that. Amen.*

Which is not to say we shouldn't ask for what we want, but even more important, we should ask God what *He* wants. Placing ourselves in service to God is the single most important key to finding right relationship with everyone and everything.

We can't save the world without God, but God can't save the world without us. In making ourselves available to His plan, we can't always see how our part fits into the overall scheme of things. But we don't need to. What we need, perhaps more than anything else, is enough faith in ourselves to appreciate His faith in us. He doesn't create small spirits, and He doesn't have small plans. He created us in greatness, and He has greatness in Mind for us. Mediocrity has no place in God's creation.

There have been times in my life when I backed away from something extraordinary, thinking, "Who am I to do such a thing?" But in reality, who was I not to do something if God had placed it in front of me? Like everything else, we have humility and arrogance completely upside down. It's not humble to think you can't do what God is asking you to do; it's arrogant to think you know yourself better than the One who thought you up.*

Whatever it is you are guided to do, don't be concerned about your own readiness; just be consistently aware of His.* Once you've asked to be the conduit through which God operates, your only job is to relax into the Holy Instant and allow the Holy Spirit to guide your thoughts and actions. We're only the faucet; God is the water.

The presence of fear is a sure sign that we're trusting in our own strength.* Once again, it's making ourselves the big deal that throws us into fear. You're not the big deal; God within you is the big deal.

Once you know that, you are so far ahead of the game.

Making Decisions

The world tells us all kinds of ways to make intelligent decisions, but there is no intelligence like Divine Intelligence. It emanates from a place in which all things past, present, and future are known and blessed. It makes decisions based on the highest good for all living things. Surrendering all decisions into the hands of God is not a giving up of personal responsibility; it is the highest form of *taking* responsibility.

When we decide things for ourselves, not only are we driving blind—unable to see around the next bend in the road—we are also trying to compensate for whatever we thought we lacked in the past. The past is a poor navigational tool. You can't steer your car forward when you're staring in the rearview mirror. Since the perception of lack then forms our core belief, we inevitably and subconsciously repeat it. Making decisions with the ego mind will only result in more ego, tightening its grip even more on our minds and on our lives.

When we place an issue in the hands of the Holy Spirit, however, He uplifts and rearranges our perceptions. When we place an issue on the altar, He alters our thinking.

I've often received direct guidance after prayerfully requesting it before going to sleep at night. If we pray at that time—"Should I do this?" or "Should I do that?"—often relevant dreams appear during our sleep, guidance may wake us during the night, or we may wake in the morning with a sense of knowing.

Those moments can be important because the ego hasn't had a chance yet to put up its mental filter and muffle the voice of God. It's odd that we teach children to say their prayers at night but somehow think that once we're adults we don't need to. Like what, once we're grown up, we know everything already so we don't need any help?

When my daughter was born, I put the name India on her birth certificate; it was the name we had decided on months before. Yet when I brought her home from the hospital, I wasn't so sure. Several names kept popping up. So the first night we were home, I prayed before I went to sleep and asked God what her name should be. I awoke the next morning with a vivid image in mind, like a clear dream just as I was waking, in which a blond little girl was holding up a white poster board with very big, clear, black letters: E M M A. I was startled, and the little girl said, "Mommy, my name is Emma." Hardly subtle.

The voice for God is like a spiritual radio signal, and late at night and first thing in the morning are when it's easiest to get clear reception—then and when we meditate. Those are the times when the world isn't so much with us, when the obfuscation of worldly plans isn't burdening our minds.

Whatever time of day it is, we can become attuned to receiving guidance that we know comes from beyond our mortal mind.

In early 1984 I was working as a temporary secretary at the World Savings Building in Los Angeles, and I had just begun lecturing on *A Course in Miracles* at the Philosophical Research Society. While a few people were coming to my lectures, I had no inkling that this would become a full-time career. As I stood at the elevator bank at work one day, I heard a voice, inside my head yet as clear as a bell, say, "This will be your last secretarial job." And other, very personal guidance has lit my way at other times. The same is true for many others I know. There are more dimensions of consciousness than the ego's worldview deems possible or real.

The voice for God doesn't ignore the realities of practical existence. The Holy Spirit understands the world yet understands its place in God's scheme of things as well. He is like an ambassador from God, entering the worldly illusion with the function of guiding us beyond it.* He shows us how to dwell on the earth while still holding on to the principles of heaven. He doesn't teach us to ignore the world or our worldly responsibilities. He simply teaches us how to live our lives with deeper meaning and in a way that serves the world best. In that way, we participate in a collective effort to reclaim this realm for love.

Many times we do hear God's guidance but we simply can't square it with what our mortal minds believe. "Why would spirit direct me to go to Chicago if Seattle is where that job is?" Only a year later will you know, and you'll feel bitterly disappointed if you missed out on something great in Chicago and find yourself saying, "I had a *feeling* I should go there!" Once you've messed up enough times because you didn't follow your inner guidance, you become much more obedient. God has only our happiness in mind—and the happiness of every living thing. Once we realize that, His path becomes much easier to follow.

Following Love

Obedience to God means a willingness to follow the dictates of love: thoughts and behavior prescribed for us by a force that wants only our happiness and good, as opposed to thoughts and behavior masquerading as our self-interest but that are in fact our own self-destructiveness.

This makes for a radical departure from a traditional notion of God as stern, frowning, judgmental, or narrow. The purpose of our lives is to be happy; God wants us to be happy, far more than we seem to want it for ourselves. It's contrary to much of traditional religious teaching to believe that surrender to God is surrender to something with only our highest good in mind. To the ego, suffering looks somehow more important, more substantial than happiness. The ego realizes that suffering changes things, but the Holy Spirit realizes that joy changes things too. Watching babies at play, are we not moved to smile? Being loved by our mate, are we not moved to smile? Achieving a creative task, are we not moved to smile? What could be more natural than joy?

Under the ego's spell, we are tempted to think, "Do I want to do God's will, or do I want to be happy?"* As long as we doubt that happiness and God's will *are the same thing*, we tend to decide against ourselves. How easy can it be to surrender if we're not convinced that what we're surrendering to really wants us to be happy?

Basing our decisions on the matters of the world should be balanced with weighing them against the matters of the heart. Once legalities, medical opinions, accounting, and other people's perspectives have been factored in; once all options have been researched and analyzed; then all decisions should be placed in the hands of God. The most powerful way to make a decision is to ask God to make it for you.*

> *Dear God,*
> *Please make this decision for me.*
> *I do not see the future,*

But You do.
I do not know what's best for everyone,
But You do.
I cannot make sense of this,
But You can.
Dear God,
Please decide this for me.
Amen.

Such a prayer authorizes spiritual forces to move mountains on your behalf. And they will.

Sometimes I feel I've asked and asked and the answer still hasn't come. At such times I know what the answer really is: as it's often said in AA, "More will be revealed." Sometimes the answer isn't as simple as "Do this" or "Do that." Sometimes it's about becoming more patient—knowing that as we continue to grow in depth and understanding, we'll either know what to do or the question will take care of itself. Only infinite patience produces immediate results.* When our faith is strong enough, we're not worried that God didn't hear us or that He might not get back to us.

And there's another issue that can tempt us to make decisions that only God should be making: our false belief that we know what is best for others. Such thoughts as "I can't leave him because he needs me" or "I have to stay in this job because the people here wouldn't be able to make it without me" are examples.

In fact, it's a win-win universe—when the Holy Spirit enters into a situation, it will be an automatic "win" for all concerned.* We are afraid to make a decision that might hurt someone, and we go around with the best of intentions trying to avoid that. Yet if we simply ask God to make our decision for us, then He who knows what is *ultimately best for everyone* will decide from a vantage point much wiser than our mortal mind could muster.

In truth, whatever God's guidance is for *you* is what would be best for others in the long run as well.

Allowing God to make our decisions is just another form of deep surrender. When God is invited to choose, more insight becomes available to us. More dimensions of knowing begin to blossom. We become so full once we make ourselves empty; we become so smart once we realize we're not; and we become so powerful once we understand we're powerless.

Exchanging our mortal intelligence for divine intelligence, we will begin to see beyond appearances. And nothing will be the same.

CHAPTER ELEVEN

From *Who We Were*
to *Who We Are Becoming*

I've often heard people say they're afraid of change. But I'm someone who grows nervous when things *don't* change. I think at times I thrive on it.

People are always walking into my house and saying, "Wait, didn't that picture used to hang in the other room?" I'm so obsessive about moving furniture (particularly pillows) around that once I actually lifted up a chair while my friend was still sitting in it!

But I have also been done in by change, overwhelmed by changes I myself set in motion, casually releasing energies that were not casual at all. I've judged certain changes to be light spring showers that turned out to be hurricanes. I have underestimated the force of change. And so I've been humbled on the subject, having learned the hard way how important it is to move slowly on the inside when things on the outside are moving fast. While I don't fear change in and of itself, I fear myself when I'm not slow and conscious and prayerful while it's happening.

In 1992 my first book, *A Return to Love*, was published. Thanks to Oprah Winfrey and her generous enthusiasm for the book, my world changed. Money came that I had never had before, along with press attention and a slight celebrity status. I didn't think of it as incredible; I just thought of it as lots to do! I became a chicken with my head chopped off, no longer taking as much time to listen, to reflect, to meditate, to think. At a time when I most needed to repair to my inner room, to ask God to enter and explain things to me, I was beginning to forget. I was moving too fast. I put some second things first and some first things second in ways I would come to regret.

I remember receiving my first royalty check, more money than I had ever seen. And perhaps particularly because I was living in Los Angeles at the time, I bought into the notion that if you have the good fortune to have money, you must buy a house. But I remember praying about this, and my guidance was clear though it seemed odd to me: "Redecorate your condo."

I kept having that thought: "Redecorate your condo." But people around me laughed at such a thought. Why would I redecorate my condo when I could afford a house? *A Course in Miracles* states that the Holy Spirit often gives guidance that sounds startling at the time, but I guess I forgot that part. I went with the voices of the world instead of the voices of my heart.

In the greater scheme of things, whether or not you purchase a house is not what matters. But it matters indeed when the voice in your heart loses volume in your head. Why was the Holy Spirit directing me to redecorate my condo? Because I needed time to adjust to the new turn my life had taken. I needed time to grow into my new circumstances, to inhabit emotionally the space I was already inhabiting materially. I needed time to think about what things meant and how to deal with new situations in the most mature way. Sometimes change lifts you up like a tornado and puts you down someplace you've never been before. Tornadoes are fast, and they are also destructive. Speed can be the enemy of constructive change.

Another reason I was being inwardly directed to remain in my condo, I think, was in order to say good-bye. I needed to say good-bye to parts of myself that were being called to transform into something new, and I needed to say hello to parts of myself that were being born. The biggest mistakes I have made in my life I would not have made had I taken more time. Time to think. And meditate. And pray.

Perhaps you were one thing and now you're another: perhaps you were in high school and now you're entering college; perhaps you were single and now you're getting married; maybe you were married and now you're single; perhaps you were childless and now you're a parent; perhaps you had a child at home and now you no longer do. Whatever door you've walked through, your life won't be quite the same as it was before. The room you were in is behind you now.

The emotional ground underneath your feet is different, and you need time to reorient yourself. Rushing through change is an unconscious move, and it's a setup for mistakes.

Navigating Change

When one stage of life gives way to another, it's the end of an era and the beginning of a new one. How we navigate such transitions spiritually will determine the joy or despair that comes next. In navigating any change, we may be tempted toward either of two extremes—resisting the change, on the one hand, or being reckless toward it, on the other. These extremes are really the flip sides of an ego-based response to change. The deeper spiritual task is to achieve moderation by avoiding both extremes.

Moderation is emotional sobriety, bringing a deep and considered awareness of both the pitfalls and the opportunities inherent in any situation. It implies a capacity for reflection, an ability to stay aware and act responsibly no matter what's occurring. Without moderation, change can be more damaging than miraculous. But no matter whether a change is happy or sad, it can be a sacred experience if we're spiritually awake.

If a change is happy, you remain awake by being grateful to God and to the people who have helped you make this happen, by remembering those who haven't been quite this lucky lately, and by not allowing yourself to get cocky or giddy. If you do, you're liable to blow it. You remain awake by praying to be worthy of your good fortune, now and always.

When a positive change is occurring in our lives, it's a good idea to take the time to sit quietly and breathe it in, literally and figuratively. In your mind's eye, see a picture of the new situation, and imagine yourself functioning at your best within it. Now with your eyes closed, breathe deeply and feel yourself inwardly expanding into that possibility within yourself. Such exercises are not idle fantasies but actual powers of the mind.

If you don't make such efforts, the ego will do everything it can to sabotage you. That, after all, is its raison d'être. Unless you firmly establish your emotional center in the midst of a new condition, you remain psychologically outside it although within it. If you're not yet dwelling within it from your own spiritual center, you'll neither take full advantage of the situation nor behave in the most centered and powerful ways. Psychic space is every bit as real—and, on a certain level, more real—than physical space. If you're *here*, and psychologically a condition is *over there*, then the split between the two will be reflected in the circumstances of your life.

Using Ritual

One of the ways to powerfully align a material circumstance with an internal reality is through ritual. We can use simple ceremony to imbue any transition with enlightened understanding.

We can do more than simply give birth to our children; we can uplift the experience of their childhood and our relationship to them through baptism, bris, a baby-naming ceremony, and so forth.

We can do more than simply watch our children grow into adolescence; we can prayerfully bid farewell to their childhood and welcome them into adulthood, uplifting this new phase of their lives through coming-of-age ceremonies, bar and bat mitzvahs, and so forth.

With ritual, we do more than simply begin a new job; we prayerfully ask that it serve God's purposes and invoke spiritual forces to support us in the effort. We do more than simply get married; we pray for God to unite our hearts, to enter the marriage and make it a blessing on the world. We do more than simply get divorced; we ask for God's help in healing our hearts, filling us with forgiveness, and paving the way for new beginnings. We do more than lose a job; we perform a ritual to ask God's help in turning this situation into a blessing, providing a higher form of abundance and service. We do more than bury our loved ones; we perform a memorial service to bring their souls, and ours, to comfort and peace in the arms of God.

In the summer of 2004, the United States officially unveiled our World War II Memorial, honoring men and women who fought valiantly for freedom in that war. A Washington memorial has more than symbolic significance; it becomes part of the psychic landscape of a nation, as we permanently enshrine the memory of those who sacrificed so much for us. Still, to have its greatest power, a memorial must be emotionally and spiritually *met* by those who visit there. In visiting the Lincoln, Jefferson, or Washington Memorials, you can feel that some people are visiting with a tourist mentality, but you can also feel the presence of those who bring with them a depth of spirit that makes their visit a civic pilgrimage. Their hearts and minds are open to sacred contact with great beings who lived before us, whom we will never meet, and yet who profoundly affected the lives we live. You can read the quotes from Jefferson or Lincoln on the sides of their memorials with mere historic interest or with a soulful immersion in the power and meaning and blessing of their lives.

Travel has great ritualistic potential. If you visit the Sphinx and the pyramids in Egypt or the Parthenon in Greece, the Mother Temple in Bali or the Glastonbury Cathedral, who you are when you go there—what consciousness you bring to the experience—will determine the depth at which the visit will affect your life.

Ritual is so instinctive within human beings that we spontaneously create it when it's needed. From people leaving millions of flowers at Kensington Palace after the death of Princess Diana to flowers and teddy bears and pictures left at the door of the late John F. Kennedy Jr.'s apartment; from the picture- and prayer- and poem-strewn fence around the Oklahoma City Murrah Federal Building bomb site to the candle-lit gathering in

New York City at which thousands prayed for the victims of the World Trade Center disaster, people know we need a vessel for our feelings—to order them, give them meaning, and spiritually lift them up.

Some rituals are collective, such as the inauguration of a president or the coronation of a monarch. The psychic rite of passage is as important as the legal one, in that it touches the heart not only of the leader but also of the people who will be led.

If someone whom I did not vote for wins an election, then my heart might not as easily acquiesce to his or her leadership. An inauguration, however, calls forth the psychological, emotional, and spiritual affirmation that I might otherwise withhold. The relationship of a people to their leader is an ancient, archetypal connection imprinted on the human psyche; a ritualistic beginning summons the heart's goodwill.

If things are good, perform a ritual to praise and thank God. If things are sad, perform a ritual to call the angels to help you endure. Either way, a ritual will envelop you in a light that no material force has the power to bestow. It is an outer event that realigns internal forces, lifting them back up to where they came from and where they belong. Holy ritual joins heaven and earth together.

Then a fractured world becomes whole again because we do.

Preparing the Heart for Change

Before I knew I was pregnant with my daughter, I walked around for days with a strong sense that everything was about to change. That's all I knew. It was only with time that the realization of just *what* was about to change made its way into my conscious awareness; when it did, there was no way for me to know—never having given birth before—what a profound and fundamental transition was under way.

When my daughter was born, I loved her, of course. But my psyche was as thrown by the experience as it was exalted. I see now that pregnancy and childbirth are rife with psychological and emotional changes just as significant as the changes occurring inside a woman's body. In a materialistically oriented culture, of course, we tend to give more credence to physical changes than to emotional ones, and that is to our detriment. "She's pregnant, so she's a little nuts right now" is hardly a profound description of a pregnant woman's psychological condition. I wish I had prepared myself inwardly for motherhood as well as I prepared my life externally. There should have been a room for her inside myself as carefully designed as the darling baby's room for her inside my apartment. Her room was painted with precious pink and white clouds, with bluebirds holding up yellow ribbons near the ceiling. But looking back, I wish I had paid more attention to the room inside my heart, where the inner dynamics of motherhood had just begun to reverberate.

How would I have done it differently? I remember a big baby shower that was held for me at the home of my girlfriend Victoria. I have a photograph of me—with those forty additional pounds of pregnancy—sitting on Victoria's couch (if you can call what you're doing at that point "sitting"), surrounded by my girlfriends just a week or so before Emma was born. The gifts they brought to me were wonderful, and I felt a lot of love. But I see now that far more serious business was at hand at that time of my life, and had I known then what I know now, I would have held a ceremony, a woman's circle, some ritualistic process to mark this extraordinary moment in the life of two females—my daughter and me. Motherhood is a mystery, neither aided nor revealed by the registry at Toys "R" Us.

When a woman gives birth, two are born: a baby is born from the womb of its mother, and a woman is born from the womb of her former existence. Physical birth more or less takes care of itself, while spiritual rebirth is an experience we must consciously cultivate.

Postpartum depression, I suspect, is an experience that does not emerge in a society devoted to the sacred. In fact, what society regards as postpartum depression is the emotional consequence of unfinished business: a woman not yet having cut the umbilical cord with the woman she used to be. The transition into motherhood involves grieving a life that must now be psychically set aside, not just to make room for a child, but to make room for a new dimension of the woman's consciousness and life experience. With every new stage of life, there are things to grieve as well as things to celebrate.

By the time my daughter reached adolescence, I was clearer about a lot of this. I made sure that both she and I held her bat mitzvah in the highest light possible. This was a transition from life as a Jewish girl to life as a Jewish woman, and I knew that, as in everything else, we could play it deep or we could play it shallow. I wanted to lay down a carpet of roses for her, leading her out of childhood and into maidenhood, then into the womanhood that lay beyond. Many women, and men as well, would be so much less wounded had someone done that for us.

I told her I would give her the fun and fancy party, but only if she did the real work. None of this memorizing a few lines of Hebrew and pretending that's the real deal.

One day she asked me what I thought the theme should be for her bat mitzvah. I said, "What do you mean, theme?"

"Oh, kids have a theme," she said. "Like, for the party. Some people have a Detroit Pistons theme or a Britney Spears theme. . . ." I thought I would faint. I said very clearly and distinctly, "The theme of your bat mitzvah is that you are becoming a woman in the eyes of God. *Period.*"

Much to her credit, my daughter understood. She studied assiduously for months with a great cantor who taught her well, and as the bat mitzvah approached, we had marvelous conversations about what this transition would mean for both of us. For her, it meant she would no longer be a child. She wouldn't be a woman either but would rather be entering a phase of her life undervalued by contemporary culture: becoming what those before us called a maiden (or for boys, a master). Without consciously honoring this period, young people often play it out like a psychic circus, with belly button rings replacing prayer beads and casual sex replacing a connection to the divine. I wanted Emma to have a sacred context for these extraordinary years. I wanted her to appropriately separate from her childhood bond to me, and for both of us to move gracefully into new dimensions of ourselves and of our relationship to each other.

During the bat mitzvah, I ceremonially gave my daughter up to God and to the world. After saying prayers on the *bima* with her, I then, like millions of Jewish women before me, took my place in the congregation and watched my child lead the rest of the service by herself. As she read from the Torah in Hebrew, the presence of God was like a glow that filled the room. And after she carried the Torah on her shoulders and placed it back in the ark, the cantor led her to me and said, "You brought her here a child. I return her to you a woman."

I never felt more power, or more love, in my life.

Torches Pass

Sometimes we perform ritual without even knowing that we're doing so. When I was an eighteen-year-old college student, I went to hear a lecture by the late author Norman O. Brown, whose book *Love's Body* had inspired me greatly. After his talk, I stood in line to ask him very earnestly if he had any advice for me. He told me the Talmudic principle that in the midst of the darkest night, we should act as if the morning has already come. And then he kissed my forehead. A feeling of complete bliss came over me that lasted for hours.

A kiss on the forehead is a power-filled gesture: someone kisses (gives love to) your forehead (your third eye, or seat of the soul). What more profound ritual could there be for sending someone off with your blessing?

During that same period I received another, equally wonderful, blast of energy. I was walking with one of my professors—now jazz critic Stanley Crouch—to attend a lecture by Jane Fonda. This was 1970 or '71, and Fonda was visiting college campuses to discuss her antiwar activism. She was gorgeous, very thin in jeans and work shirt, wearing the layered haircut she made famous in the movie *Klute*. And she looked like she was lit from within. The combination of her stunning physical beauty and her almost spiritual radiance blew me away then and still does when I think about it. And while she was walking to the lecture, she did something that changed my life.

Crouch, who is African American, and I were walking down a sidewalk perpendicular to the one she was strolling on. As she crossed our sidewalk, she turned her head and glanced at us. I don't know what made her face light up—young white female walking with black professor? (remember, this was 1970)—but she then shot a smile in my direction that rivaled in power the transmissions of energy I received years later from a spiritual master. She seemed to project some wonderfulness onto Stanley's and my merely walking together, and her approval hit me like a tidal wave of positive energy. From that point forward, it felt like I had been blessed by Jane Fonda.

I wanted to mention this incident when I met Fonda almost thirty years later, but I didn't. I would have felt stupid. What was I supposed to say: "I saw you thirty years ago, and there was light pouring out of your head, and when you smiled at me I felt like a thunderbolt had hit my chest and I knew I was okay"? That moment had clearly passed. But I had been given a gift that would stay with me forever because my choices—or at least one of my choices, on some level symbolizing many others—had been validated by a woman of power.

Today many young women come up to me at my lectures, and I see in them the young woman I once was. They tell me they want to do what I do, and I'm sure they will—only better. A torch is always being passed from one generation to the next. My speaking might have lit some star in their sky the way other women have lit stars in mine. All of us are passing from one state to another all the time, and God sends guides and angels, inspirers and mentors, to light our way. He is always, always preparing new life.

The In-between Times

Sometimes we are living in the in-between times: when we're no longer who we used to be, but we haven't yet arrived at our next stage either.

In January 2004, I took my daughter to see Bette Midler perform; for me, this was the third time. I remembered seeing her
perform in New York City in the seventies and then again in Los
Angeles in the early nineties. The years had passed and so much
had changed. Taking my daughter to see the show, I felt like I was
passing on to her a beautiful gift that had meant a lot to me.
Midler's music had stirred my soul, and now it would perhaps
stir hers.

It was interesting to see how Bette had changed and how she
had not changed. On one hand, jokes that played well ten or
twenty-five years ago do not play the same way now: the world is
entirely different, and so are we. But the change that I noticed
most was in Midler herself. She clearly cares deeply about people
and is herself a very serious person; her commentary on the state
of the world, and in particular American politics, was searing
and real. (It was courageous even, given that some in her audience
would surely not have agreed with her!) Yet I could sense an
angst in her that seemed to me a poignant reflection of the state
of our generation. We're still telling jokes, but nothing seems all
that funny anymore.

What the evening impressed upon me was that we can't go
home again. The seventies, eighties, and nineties of the divine
Miss M no longer exist. They were a fun point in time, like a
really cool party. But the party has ended, and the world, as she
pointed out, is no longer safe for any of us. We were like children
in those days, and we are children no more. I sensed she was not
entirely kidding when she said she had taken a couple of years
off to suffer through her menopause in silence.

Midler really didn't seem able to throw herself heart and soul
into the old jokes. How could she? I could imagine her arguing

with someone on her production team: "Oh come on, Bette. Those jokes are still funny! That routine still works! There's a whole new audience out there that hasn't heard this stuff yet, and they'll love it!" Her response—at least in my imagination— would be that she's too sick about the state of the world to do those jokes anymore. How can we laugh like that when the world is so messed up? Bette Midler lit up only two times during the night: When she was dead serious about politics and the state of the world and when she was singing songs that were musically profound.

I could see her conundrum, because she—like so many of us—is neither here nor there. She is no longer who she was (though she can mimic it brilliantly)—but she is not yet who she is becoming. She can *do* the other things still—Delores the Fish and Clementine and Ernie—but I sensed they weren't quite as true to her soul anymore. Perhaps this is all my projection, but it was how I felt. She, like so many of us, now seems in a middle zone, where real change happens. We are spiritually too big at this point to fit into the attitudinal clothes we used to wear, yet the new ones are still hanging in the closet.

When you take off one set of clothes, you are naked for a minute before you put on another. When age is seen in a purely material context, you sort of wonder if there *is* another set of clothes. Yet in a spiritual context, there is no phase of life— because there is no point in the universe—where God is not. We are always on the road to the next stage, whether we are days old or decades old. The spirit of life is not diminished by time. In the present moment, our task is to let go of what was, with love or even sorrow, and embrace what emerges next from the Mind of God. When we have seen the world and understood the world and felt our souls grow sick of the world, it's time for us to become children again. We look to God to give us new life when the old one has begun to die.

I'd go see Midler's brilliance anytime, but I have a distinct impression that the next time I see her, Clementine and Ernie might have morphed into something new. She has already demonstrated theatrical greatness and now seems headed toward our generational destiny: a greatness that will be the crowning glory of all her achievements up until this point, paving the way for the transformation of our world. Shakespeare said all the world's a stage, and all of us players on it. Today—whether we are famous entertainers or just regular folks—it feels like years of rehearsal are finally over, and the greatest performance of our lives is about to begin.

Playing Our Part

There was a time when the thought of changing the world didn't really seem all that hard.

When you're young, it's fairly easy to embrace the notion that we will someday cast away all problems from the world. Our bodies are young and voluptuous, our energy endless, our opportunities seemingly infinite; we think it's only a matter of time before all problems will bow before the power of our efforts (which are, after all, so impressive). Yet life has a way of wearing you down. You learn through often painful means that in the face of your prodigious intellect and energy, evil does not just step aside. It's tempting to succumb to the cynicism of age when you see how often things do not change. Especially when the most recalcitrant factors, the most immovable mountains, seem to be within yourself.

How can I believe the whole world will change its neurotic patterns when I keep marrying the same person over and over again? How can I believe two nations that keep murdering each other's citizens are going to find peace anytime soon when I'm still not talking to my parents?

Our attitudinal, not just our physical, muscles become less flexible with age. It's amazing how much fatigue enough disappointments can cause. It takes energy to change, and sometimes our energy is in short supply. You can feel the pressure, once you reach middle age, to simply go along with a status quo that is hardly what you hoped for but is here, so what the hell.

Jesus said of Lazarus, "He is not dead. He is only sleeping." And so are we. There lies in most of us the accumulated frustration of our unlived dreams and the squelched desire to spread our wings and fly above the worldly limitations that hold us back. These painful energies are not automatically transmuted except through prayer and surrender and holy relationships. They attach themselves to our spiritual organs of faith and hope, taunting us with lines like "You're too old" or "You blew it" or "You're washed up." And at times they seem to be backed by evidence.

To say to those voices, "Satan, get thee behind me," is not mumbo jumbo or wishful thinking. Spiritually, it's our power and our strength.

Angels and Demons

During the wee hours of the morning, both angels and demons take shape. The glories of a life as well as its terrors are clearer before dawn has broken. Once the light of day casts its spell upon us, deeper meanings—sometimes obvious only hours before—are easily forgotten. We fall prey to the mind-set of the world.

How unnatural our modern Western relationship to nature's clock. Did Edison realize the havoc that lay hidden in his gift to humanity? The electric lightbulb would change the world. In service to the industrial era and its demands for productivity, we trained ourselves to sleep when the system needed us to sleep and to wake when it needed us to awaken. How often, then, we miss the sunrise and its simple blessings. These blessings are not metaphorical. They are more than merely beautiful; they are a reminder from God: "Look what I bring forth out of every dark night; such is the work I shall do within you."

Growing older is a form of night, full of angels and demons as well. We are closer to wisdom, yet we are closer to death. It takes a lot of climbing to get a clear perspective: climbing above the thoughts and feelings that would keep us tied to the ground we have trod before. The ground of yesterday is barren now. Its drama is over. Only the present, lived in fullness and intensity, holds the promise of a new tomorrow.

Night after night, I have lain awake, my eyes having popped open for no apparent reason, my body unwilling to fall back asleep, my hormones not feeling like they are mine anymore. For a while, I said the usual things to myself: "I hate this; I must have my estrogen checked again; I need to buy more melatonin; this will feel so awful tomorrow." Yet finally I noticed that more was going on: "I'm that age, so I'm having a hard time sleeping" was such a hand-me-down notion, so devoid of dimension, so superficial in its interpretation of my own experience. From a spiritual perspective, these hours were not tired; they were deeply awake. The rest we seek we will find not from sleeping but from waking.*

In those hours that I've lain so inconveniently awake, I think I've begun at last to know what awakened means. Noting the witching hour—4:15—at which I awake more often than not, stealing outside to look at the stars and marvel at the moon, I return again to my ancient self. In those hours, I am not a menopausal nutcase. I'm a magical witch, and I can feel it in my bones.

WHEN ASPECTS OF YOU that used to work have peaked now; when situations that used to seem exciting have lost their edge, and so have you; when a phrase like "over the hill" suddenly means something after all, then you are ready for rebirth. It is time to face the terrifying void—not in resignation but in faith. For this void is the womb for a new emerging self. From the acid of regrets over things that did and did not happen to our tenacious hopes for what might yet still occur, a profound, transformative alchemy is at work within us. We are not done—not until God rings the bell.

And that bell, as we know, might be far, far off. A television interviewer once asked Clint Eastwood about his marriage to a woman decades younger than he. I loved his wry answer: "If she dies, she dies!" Indeed, who knows who is leaving when? In 1994, my sister died at the age of forty-four. The next year, my father died at eighty-five. Go figure.

So what are we to do with the rest of our lives should we choose a path of spiritual rebirth? First, we must *consciously choose to live them.* Hidden beliefs are dangerous, and the belief that "the best years of my life are behind me" is a powerful agent—not of change, but of inertia. Whether or not we consciously embrace the thought, many of us do think it. And thoughts like that can be changed.

If we primarily identify with external realities, as we've been trained to do by the ego's thought system, then it's hard to look forward to better years after a certain number of them have passed. Yet this is our challenge: to see beyond the world and thus invoke new beginnings. A child grows whether or not he or she chooses to. At a certain point in life, however, we grow *only* if we choose to. And in that choice lies a choice not only for ourselves but indeed for everyone.

Deeper with the Years

Visiting London in the fall of 2003, I went to the Royal Academy of Arts to view Andrew Lloyd Webber's collection of Pre-Raphaelite paintings. One of them, a picture called *Silver and Gold*, shows a beautiful young woman walking with an elderly lady. I stared at the painting for quite a while, remembering what it was like to be the young woman in the picture, like a part I had acted in a play that had closed and would not be opening again. I'm certainly not yet the elderly woman but rather I'm perched somewhere between the two. I can now relate to the older woman I will hopefully be someday as much as to the younger woman I no longer am. And what is striking about the picture, to me, is the seriousness with which the older woman is listening to the younger one. Is the younger one her granddaughter? Her charge? One doesn't know. But she clearly cares about the younger woman, who seems to be drinking in her attention. It is part of the younger woman's initiation into the mysteries, that she experiences the goodwill of a woman who has passed through her own youth and now cares about someone else's.

My mother once said to me, "You know, Marianne, whatever age you are, you experienced all the ages before it." She had probably said that in response to something I had patronizingly said, indicating that youth was something she couldn't possibly understand! And my father, at around the age of eighty, said to me, "It's funny. When you're old, you don't *feel* old." My conclusion is that age, while in an eternal sense is truly nothing, in a material sense is truly something. And I honor both, since both are mine.

I had a personal assistant who was twenty years younger than me, and sometimes when I would see her coming down the hall I would swear I was looking at a younger version of myself. I enjoyed her joy at things I hardly even noticed anymore—her amazement that Cameron Diaz makes more than *two million dollars!* to star in a movie, and her excitement about going to Paris for the first time. Watching her was like a chance to say hello to a me I no longer was. And I knew she too was staring down a hall toward a woman she might one day be.

I once had a friend who was dying of cancer, and after her death I began dating her boyfriend. He told me that during the last few months of her life her sessions in therapy often centered on her intuitive sense that one day he and I would be together. She had to deal with the fact that the arc of her life was winding down while on a certain level mine was just starting up. It pained me to think of what she must have felt. And now, having entered the last half of my life, I realize more and more what she was letting go.

None of us has control of the parts we're cast in during the ever-changing drama of life. You're the young Turk when you're the young Turk; you're the aging crone when you're the aging crone; you're the innocent in love when you're the innocent in love; and you're jaded when you're jaded. Yet something in us is none of those things; who we truly are is changeless in the Mind of God. We're just experiencing different corners of the universe, to learn its dimensions, its lessons, before going on to another. I don't think death is the end of our lives, for as surely as we're headed out of here we're heading toward some new adventure. I assume the wheel of karma keeps turning until every point God wanted to make He's had a chance to make, and He can see we got them all.

It's important to give up yesteryear when yesteryear is gone. I remember complaining to my best friend that when I lecture, I'm not as fast as I once was, not as snap-crackle-and-pop in my delivery. His response was helpful: that many in my audience aren't as fast now either, that they too are no longer as snap-crackle-and-pop, and it would seem disingenuous if I tried to be. Age slows us down, but it takes us deeper, into realms no less fertile, spiritually, than those we inhabited before. As the years go by, we lose some of the outer sparkle that so gloriously infused our youth—but an inner sparkle emerges that we never before had. Ralph Waldo Emerson wrote, "As I age, my beauty steals inward."

And it's more than just our beauty that steals inward. The entire richness of life begins to burrow underground as we age; no less magical, just not as visible to the physical eye. In fact, in a way, life becomes more magical. For magic is of the invisible planes.

Thinking about my young assistant's excitement about going to Paris for the first time, I thought about my history with that city vis-à-vis the men I've known. The years that take a woman from youth to maturity are marked emotionally by her history in love. There are phases of Paris, like there are phases of certain relationships: getting ready for it, being there, and remembering what it was like.

When I was young, I once went to Paris with a man who enchanted me as much as the city did. Our efforts to make the trip happen and the times we had there once we did are memories I'll hold dear forever. But decades later, there was another man. And when the subject of Paris came up between us, one quick glance said it all.

Both of us had been there, I could tell, and both of us had loved there; I could feel it. Both of us had had dreams come true there, and both of us had dreams that died there. We didn't even have to have the discussion, so clear it was in that one split-second glance that both of us knew all sides of it. I realized then that where we had gone in that moment—not in spite of the years we'd lived but clearly because of them—was a place more enchanting than Paris.

A New Future Begins

And what of those who say, "Well, maybe we could change the world—but not in my lifetime. So why should I try?"

According to Buddhism, it is not what we achieve in our lives but what we at least die *trying* to achieve that gives meaning to our existence. Susan B. Anthony never lived to see the passage of the Nineteenth Amendment. Yet millions of women live infinitely more empowered lives because of her. Her tireless efforts for generations of women she would never know provided half of all Americans—and I think the other half as well—with a greater capacity to express themselves fully. Surely, on some heavenly level, her soul receives the blessing she gave.

And now, in our time and through our efforts, we too are called to a great vision: to think the thoughts of a world at peace, infused with total love. For until we think the thoughts of peace, peace will not be ours. We will end war not because we hate it so much; we will end it by loving peace so much more. We will love it enough to try to live it in our own lives. We can wage a preemptive peace, in our hearts and in our politics. And then one day we will notice that war has disappeared.

Years from now, when we ourselves are no longer remembered, people will live on a peaceful planet, not knowing whom to bless, not knowing whom to thank. Children will ask their parents, "Is it true that there was once a time when people had wars?" And the parents will say, "Yes, there was such a time. But a very long time ago. Wars don't happen anymore."

And when that happens, surely on some level our souls will receive the blessing we gave. We will lift our glasses to the heaven we are already in, and with both tears and laughter we will howl, "We did it!"

NO MATTER WHO YOU ARE or what you have done, God is aware if you are willing to work on His behalf. If you have stumbled and then gotten back up—whether you stumbled through your own doing or someone else's intent to harm you or both—you will arise now with new power. You will speak with deeper credibility and carry a deeper compassion for those who suffer. You will have gained wisdom and humility and will never again be as easily tricked by the ego. You are further prepared for service to God.

This is a time in all our lives to deal with those issues that we have pushed into the back of a drawer, that keep us from performing at less than 100 percent. This is the time for us to make a radical break from our weaker selves, devoting each day to the total elimination of whatever ego energies remain attached to our psyches to ruin our lives. This cannot be done without prayer. It cannot be done without work. It cannot be done without brutal self-honesty. It cannot be done without forgiving self and others. It cannot be done without love. But when it is done, we achieve spiritual mastery. The rock in front of our tomb is removed. Our spirit resurrects, and we are ready for the light. We are ready in the sense that we can contain it now: We have come at last to live in the comfort of our own skin.

We realize the huge calling of history at this time. We have been called to a collective genius, and each of us is being prepared to play our part. Our world needs spiritual giants, and it takes not ego but humility to sign up for the effort. Many of our problems arose because we chose to play small, thinking there we would find safety. But we were born with wings, and we are meant to spread them. Anything less will hurt us, will deny love to ourselves and others, and will mean that we end our lives not having flown the flight of spiritual glory.

Let us fly.

> *Dear God,*
> *If left to my own devices,*
> *my perceptions will be skewed.*
> *I surrender to You everything I think and feel.*
> *Please take my past, and plan my future.*
> *Send Your Spirit to redeem my mind,*
> *that I might be set free.*

May I be Your vessel
And serve the world.
May I become who You would have me be,
that I might do what You would have me do.
And I will, dear God.
Amen.

Now imagine yourself as you would like to be. Close your eyes and see yourself as elegant, dignified, and calm. See yourself as smart, insightful, humble, and kind. Imagine all your weaknesses replaced by strength. And do not stop. Remain in stillness with your eyes closed for as long as you can, for you are conceiving new life. Ask the Spirit of God to come into you and give you birth into the fullness of your possible self. Whatever the portal through which you enter the house of God, know that His house is where you are truly at home. It is where you will find who you are, receive repair of your soul, heal from the world, and begin again. You will go back into the darkness of the world and bring to it your light. You will have experienced a miracle, and through you others will experience miracles too.

God so loves you, and loves the world, that He is sending it the person He has created you to be.

Remember that in any situation, only what you are not giving can be lacking. Bring the love of God, and you will bless all things. He will be at your left, and He will be at your right. He will be in front of you, and He will be behind you. Wherever you go, He will be there with you.

And together, you will change the world.

For information about my books, lectures, and classes, please check my Web site, *www.marianne.com.*
You will also find my audio recordings, which can be downloaded to your iPod or MP3 player.

Going from Here

*F*or those of you who would like to follow up on studying *A Course in Miracles,* you might appreciate the following resources:

1. My book *A Return to Love* is like a primer on *A Course in Miracles.*
2. *The Circle of Atonement* offers a wide range of teaching materials designed to help the student walk this transformative path. Headed up by Robert Perry, author of *Path of Light: Stepping into Peace with* A Course in Miracles, the Circle is one of the most internationally respected voices among Course students. It offers a vision of *A Course in Miracles* that is both faithful to the Course and practical for the student. Visit the Circle's Web site at *www.circleofa.com* to access a wealth of free materials.

Contact:
The Circle of Atonement
P.O. Box 4238
W. Sedona, AZ 86340
Phone: 928-282-0790
E-mail: info@circleofa.com
www.circleofa.com

3. Since 1978, Miracle Distribution Center has been the world-wide contact point for students of *A Course in Miracles*, supporting their understanding and integration of the Course's principles into daily life. President Beverly Hutchinson is a gracious presence within the Course community. Services include *The Holy Encounter*, a free bimonthly magazine with inspirational and educational articles on the Course; international Course study group listings; weekly recorded classes on the Course; worldwide prayer ministry; international Course conferences and retreats; mail-order and online catalog service; counseling referral service; and an interactive Web site that includes chat and live monthly webcasts. Most importantly, the center can fill you in on other Course activities going on throughout the world.

Contact:
Miracle Distribution Center
3947 E. La Palma Ave.
Anaheim, CA 92807
Phone: 800-359-2246
www.miraclecenter.org

4. Any work by Dr. Gerald Jampolsky is wonderful. He and his wife, Diane Cirincione, founded the Center for Attitudinal Healing in 1975. Attitudinal healing is a process based on *A Course in Miracles*, teaching that in every moment we can choose love over fear, peace rather than conflict, and experience the peace that forgiveness brings. The Centers for Attitudinal Healing are an international network dealing with illness and dying, loss and grief, but also with anyone who wishes to heal a relationship and live life to the fullest.

Contact:

The Center for Attitudinal Healing

33 Buchanan Dr.

Sausalito, CA 94965

Phone: 415-331-6161

E-mail: home123@aol.com

www.healingcenter.org or *www.attitudinalhealing.org*

5. Aeesha and Kokomon Clottey do marvelous work applying the principles of *A Course in Miracles* to racial healing. They are coauthors of a book called *Beyond Fear: Twelve Spiritual Keys to Racial Healing*, and their Racial Healing groups take place at the Attitudinal Healing Connection in Oakland, California, the last Wednesday of every month.

Contact:

The Attitudinal Healing Connection

3278 West St.

Oakland, CA 94608

Phone: 510-652-7901

www.ahc-oakland.org

S P E C I A L   O F F E R

Order these selected Thorsons and Element titles direct from the publisher and receive £1 off each title! Visit www.thorsonselement.com for additional special offers.

Free post and packaging for UK delivery (overseas and Ireland, £2.00 per book).

Liberation Barefoot Doctor (0 00 716510 2)	£7.99 – £1.00 = £6.99
The Success Principles Jack Canfield (0 00 719508 7)	£12.99 – £1.00 =£11.99
The Alchemist Paulo Coelho (0 7225 3293 8)	£6.99 – £1.00 = £5.99
The Monk Who Sold His Ferrari Robin Sharma (0 00 717973 1)	£7.99 – £1.00 = £6.99

Place your order by post, phone, fax, or email, listed below. Be certain to quote reference code **714W** to take advantage of this special offer.

Mail Order Dept. (REF: **714W**)   Email: customerservices@harpercollins.co.uk
HarperCollins*Publishers*   Phone: 0870 787 1724
Westerhill Road   Fax: 0870 787 1725
Bishopbriggs G64 2QT

Credit cards and cheques are accepted. Do not send cash. Prices shown above were correct at time of press. Prices and availability are subject to change without notice.

BLOCK CAPITALS PLEASE

Name of cardholder   _____
Address of cardholder   _____
                          _____
                          _____
Postcode   _____

Delivery address (if different)
                          _____
                          _____
                          _____
Postcode   _____

I've enclosed a cheque for £_____, made payable to HarperCollins*Publishers*, or please charge my Visa/MasterCard/Switch (circle as appropriate)

Card Number: _____
Expires: __/__   Issue No: __/__   Start
Date: __/__
Switch cards need an issue number or start date validation.

Signature:_____

Make www.thorsonselement.com your online sanctuary

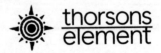